PRAISE FOR DOGGYALITY

"Larry Fine's amazing training skills have helped innumerable pets and their people become stronger communicators and better teams. With his deep understanding of the canine mind and his passion for effective and safe training practices, Larry has blossomed into one of our area's best-known and most respected trainers. His passion for effective and safe training practices, and his talent for sharing information in an enjoyable way, has resulted in many pets staying in foster homes that seemed impossible, and fixing problems that seemed unfixable. I am so pleased that Larry has finally written down his wealth of knowledge to be shared with the world!"

—Buzz Miller, Founder and President of PACT for Animals, a national nonprofit that fosters companion animals for members of our country's military personnel and hospital patients of all ages who are unable to care for the pets they love.

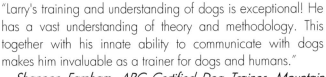

"Larry Fine gets into the heart and minds of dogs everywhere. His methods create confident owners and dogs because he is able to capture the essential brainwork of a dog and convey that to owners. His progressive style is much needed in today's training." *—Tasley Wheeler, Dog Trainer, Jacksonville, FL*

"Larry's training and understanding of dogs is exceptional! He has a vast understanding of theory and methodology. This together with his innate ability to communicate with dogs makes him invaluable as a trainer for dogs and humans."

—Shannon Farnham, ABC Certified Dog Trainer, Mountain Paws, Winthrop, WA

"When I brought a 14–year–old beagle into my home, she attacked my other dogs. I had pretty much given up hope of her ever being allowed to roam free with the others, and made one last–ditch plea to The Old Dog House in Jacksonville for any suggestions. They put me in touch with Larry Fine. In just a few weeks of training them all together, we made huge steps!" *—Susan McHenry, Baldwin, NY*

"We found Larry after another trainer referred him to one of our placements in the Northeast. He got through to this dog immediately and has already helped several of our cases. We are hoping Larry can include Memphis in his Southern tour this year." *—Donna Quick, Bailey's Arms Dog Rescue, Memphis, TN*

"Thanks to Larry, our dogs are doing well. It's been a year since their last really bad fight. We have adjusted and they are getting better and better since using the Doggyality method." *—Ginger Snap, Silver Spring, MD*

"Larry's methods are excellent! His calm demeanor put my four behaviorally challenged dogs instantly at ease. They immediately responded to Larry's training method and understood what was being asked of them. The results have stood the test of time and have helped create a calmer and happier home for my pack of misfits. I learned a lot from Larry. His methods are refreshing and have helped me in my own practice."
—Jessica Rosman, ABC Certified Dog Trainer, Charlotte, NC

DOGGYALITY
COGNITIVE TRAINING FOR **DOGS & HUMANS**

Larry Fine

Doggyality LLC
www.doggyality.com

Doggyality: Cognitive Training for Dogs & Humans

Inquiries may be sent to:
Doggyality LLC
P.O. Box 191, Merion Station, PA 19066
Email: info@doggyality.com

Published in the United States of America by Doggyality LLC

ISBN–13: 978-1512322989
ISBN–10: 1512322989

Graphics and cover design by Lee Kancher
(www.rightbraingroup.com)
Interior design by Bruce Kluger

Cover and selected interior photos by Kristin Flagg
(www.indigoskyworld.com)
All other photos courtesy of Larry Fine

Edited by David Tabatsky

To my wonderful clients and their happy dogs.
With your trust and dedication,
we have proven a better way
to interact with our best friends.
All of our lives are better for it.

In memory of Captain David O. Schwartz,
the man who defined the term "Won't Quit."

CONTENTS

Foreword by Kelly Meerbott   v

Introduction: Birth of a New Man   vii

The Doggyality Cast of Characters   xi

The Doggyality Method   xiv
Acknowledging the Status Quo • What About Human
Accountability? • A Trainer's Belligerence • The Beauty
of Blocking • A Client's Testimonial • Dogs According to
Wendy Kaplan • Finding the Trainer in Each of Us

Part One: The Cognitive Process   1
My Learning Curve with Dude • Strategies for Success •
The Stay Command • Training Integration • Run Away
Recall • Turning Everyday Interactions into Training
Exercises • Controlling You Before Your Dog • Using
Non–Verbal Communication • The Magic of Distraction
• The Science of Decision–Making • Converting Threat
to Opportunity • ETOP in the Extreme • Alicia
Harantschuk's Passion for Pet Therapy • Reflex Versus
Thought Process • Cause and Effect Versus Logic and
Reason • "Stay" Is a State of Mind • What If We Were
More Like Dogs? • Homer's Odyssey • What I've
Learned from Dogs

Part Two: Puppies, Rescues and Special Needs   37

GPS: Guide Pooch Straight • Teaching Basic Commands: Physical Prompting, Luring, Behavior Capture • Word to Action Versus Action to Word • Three Forms of Compliance • Mental Impressions • Conditioning Behavior Through Cause and Effect • Case Study: Shamus Meets a New Dog • Welcome to the World of Puppies and Rescue • Interactions with Dogs • Puppy Proofing • Puppy Meets Crate • Teaching Potty Training • The Puppy Journal: A Daily Sample • The Ebb–and–Flow of Breaking a Comfort Zone • But It's A Rescue • Doggyality Is Not Just for Dogs! • Welcome to Humanality 101 • Let Sleeping Dogs Lie • Every Dude Has a Past • Empathy and Allelomimetic Behaviors • My Four–Legged Nurse • Monkey See, Monkey Do • New Kid on the Block • Touch–Testing and the Feeding Ritual • It's a Family Affair! • The Doggyality Exercise Chart

Part Three: Happy Human, Happy Dog   73

Happy Dog, Happy Human? • Who Is Your Dog? • Energy Shifts and Standoffs • Energy Shifts with Dogs • Beryl Eismeier Learns To Do "Nothing" • Stuck On Words • Warning: Three Words You May Not Want to Hear • Learn To Love Your Walk

Conclusion: When Personality Meets Doggyality   87

Take Five—Actually, Take Ten • Jenn Shaw Gets It • Happiness is Cassidy's Ranch

Acknowledgments   93

About the Author   95

FOREWORD

Being the co–owner of two large female dogs, a mixed breed and a golden retriever, I am no stranger to dog training. Over the past ten years, I've experienced my share of trick trainers, militant trainers, doggy boot camps, Marker Training, Lure/Reward Training, Compulsion/Praise Training and dog behaviorists.

I am happy to say that Larry Fine's work is unlike anything I've ever seen.

It all starts with how he shows up.

As he first crossed the threshold of our home, the collective energy shifted. Someone had arrived; someone with the ability to add to the positive energy, not detract from it. The change was palpable. We all could feel it, including our dogs, Jasmine (14) and Murphy (8.5).

Whoever said, "You can't teach an old dog new tricks" hasn't met Larry Fine.

Larry brought "it" with him. That's just how it is with him. It's not anything he does or does not do. It's who he inherently is, the essence of his DNA.

Larry radiates peace as he enters a space. He approached our dogs without a sound, placed himself in a position of calm respect and used his body to get Murphy to do what he wanted. There was no talking. No touching. No sound of any kind. Just the sound of deep breaths to reinforce what Larry wanted from Murphy. It was simply amazing. The only thing I can compare it to is meditation. He shifted our dogs' mindsets with simple breath and peaceful energy.

—Kelly Meerbott

Kelly is a leadership coach and the principal of You: Loud & Clear, Inc. She implements long-term, positive behavior change for successful leaders, their teams and their organizations. For more information, please visit www.youloudandclear.com.

INTRODUCTION
Birth of a New Man

My personal transformation—from energy–taker to energy–giver—started with a brindle Boxer named Cassidy. She was an abuse case rescued by a local Philadelphia group. I was asked to watch her for a few days until a foster home could be found. I was told that Cassidy would be no bother, but that she was very shook–up and not trusting of humans, sitting in the corner and shaking from time to time. At that point in my life, I was still recovering from some traumatic events of my own. I wasn't eating properly and sleep came an hour or so at a time, often in fits and frequently waking me up, frightened and perspiring. I remember laughing as I thought of myself stuck in my own corner, shaking from time to time.

When Cassidy arrived, she sat in her corner, as predicted, and I gave her plenty of space. I wasn't a dog trainer yet and knew nothing of dog psychology, but it just felt like the right thing to do. Several hours passed before she became curious about me, before she finally found the courage to come lay down on the floor near me. I didn't extend a hand or offer any gesture of reassurance. A half an hour later, Cassidy rested her chin on the couch and looked up at me.

This was my first experience with a Boxer and to be honest, I kind of thought she was ugly. But it seemed like she wanted to come up on the couch so I invited her to join me and she happily accepted. She rested her head on my lap and let out a deep sigh. I found her breathing to be extremely relaxing. I soon fell asleep and woke up several hours later. As I looked down at this sweet dog still there beside me, I laughed as I became aware of myself noticing how beautiful she was. It took a few minutes to realize, but I felt great, refreshed, and very hungry.

This brindle Boxer named Cassidy had just let years of pent up stress disappear in a mere five hours—both hers and mine! Even more amazing, Cassidy seemed at total ease. She began eating the food I left out for her. Then she slapped her front paws down but kept her rear end high. Her little nubby tail was moving like it had a motor. She was happy and she wanted to play.

Years later, I would learn that slapping the paws down in that manner is called a play bow, and her eating was a sign that she wasn't in distress anymore.

That's not all I learned.

It's also a matter of what happens when personality meets *doggy*ality.

I have an innate ability to connect with most dogs, and my natural energy vibes very well with canine energy. I had something to offer Cassidy. And she reciprocated with something I needed. Our bond that day helped us both move forward. If I had tried to approach her before she was ready, she may not have trusted me, she may have even bitten me. If I used logic and reason, tools of the human world, she would not have felt secure. My attempt to reassure her would have been perceived with uncertainty, pushing her deeper into her shell. By showing patience and allowing her to adjust at her own at her own pace, she saw a leadership quality. That's when she felt secure enough to approach me. By allowing her to be in my space and still offering no gestures, she became even more comfortable. It's so counter-intuitive, but it makes perfect sense. I earned her trust, and felt empowered.

"Cassidy," I said, succumbing to my penchant for cheesy Hollywood quotes, "I think this is the beginning of a beautiful friendship."

But I'm not the only goofball in the universe. My cousin Jeff and his wife Yael own and operate a canine behavior center in Ra'anana, Israel called Howlywood.

In January 2010, I decided to take a vacation and visit Jeff. He and I have always been close despite the distance and I wanted to play with all of his dogs. Something amazing happened on the first day I arrived. Jeff directed me to the pen and invited me to enter. I was a bit overwhelmed with the idea of going in there with close to 20 dogs. I trusted that my cousin would not be sending me into a mauling so I took a deep breath and opened the gate. My approach was relaxed, and the dogs felt it. I was comfortable and they were responsive.

The energy shift was the key, as I later came to understand much more about the relationship of human energy and dog behavior. During my short time with Jeff and Yael, I learned the basics of dog training and the psychological differences between humans and dogs. I returned to Philadelphia inspired to pursue dog training.

A month later, my sweet brindle Boxer Cassidy abruptly passed away. We were hiking in one of our favorite spots when her heart failed. I carried her out of the woods and tried to get her to a vet but I knew it was too late. She was happy right up until the second she died. She didn't feel any pain. After overcoming a tough start in her life, Cassidy had enjoyed a great life.

I was devastated, but I also felt a profound sense of peace unfold during my time of mourning. The seven great years I spent with Cassidy had changed my life. She had set me on a path that would lead to enormous personal growth and happiness. In most forms of spiritual belief, it's generally agreed that everything on this planet is here for a reason. In my opinion, dogs are on this earth to make us better people. I believe Cassidy went over the bridge in peace, knowing she did her job. She helped pick me up, dust me off, and get me back in the game. When I found my calling during that trip to Israel, she could rest easy.

According to Jeff and Yael, "At Howlywood, your dog is the star."

What does every star need for a great performance? A good director—also known as the client. The director also needs resources to get a project off the ground and that's where the producer—also known as the trainer—comes into the picture. This cast and crew scenario defines the roles we play in a dog's development.

So let me introduce the cast and crew of this Doggyality production.

My Personal Dogs

Cassie (below, right), a female Boxer, became available for adoption in April 2010, a month after Cassidy's passing. I was ready for another dog. A dominant/territorial Boxer was as good a case zero as I could ask for. As I molded Cassie into a very happy and fulfilled dog, she gave me the confidence to make my dog training business official. I launched in November 2010 with an emphasis on dog psychology, so I wanted a name that was both appropriate and cute. I had often heard people say that their dog has a great personality. But since it's a dog, not a person, doesn't it have a doggyality? And there it was.

Shamus (above, left) came into my life when I was asked to meet him for a re–home evaluation in 2011. Within fifteen minutes, I knew he should be with me. It wasn't a case of wanting him because he was so cute. It was more like I *had* to have him. I recognized right away that this dog had the ability to help other dogs. I just knew it. Five weeks later, Shamus helped me with Cooper, who had dog aggression. Cooper was so reactionary when he saw Shamus that he bit me in the hope that I would let go of him. But every time Cooper aggressed, Shamus just sat there with a very relaxed attitude. Sometimes, he would plop over and roll on his back as a gesture of trust. His patience gave Cooper time to adjust without elevating the situation and 45 minutes later they were playing off leash together in a fenced yard.

Shamus has taught me so much about how dogs interact. I knew what blocking was, but to watch Shamus do it with other dogs showed me its true value in terms of communication. Shamus taught me that dominance is not about intensity; it's about a relaxed and confident state of mind. We will explore that more in *The Doggyality Method*.

The Doggiality Cast of Characters
also includes (opposite, clockwise from top):
Cali and Harley (Marie Hallock, human),
Olivia and Vegas (Alicia Harantschuk, human),
Macy (Jennifer Shaw, human),
Dude (Dori Cohen, human),
Homer (Sara Shack, human),
Luna (Beryl Eismeier, human),
and Shay (Wendy Kaplan, human).

The
DOGGYaLITY
METHOD

More and more, we are finding out that dogs have cognitive abilities far beyond what was originally thought. When dogs fail to become well adjusted it is usually a result of human error and/or poor communication. By applying human psychology, which is confusing to dogs, we set the stage for counter–productive behavior. Instead of asking dogs to assimilate to our world, we should be meeting them half way. That means learning more about what the world is like from their perspective. Once we do that, we can help them adjust in a manner that is consistent with their strengths and abilities. And since each dog is an individual, there is no perfect formula or one–size–fits–all technique that will work for every dog.

Acknowledging the Status Quo

Most dog trainers learn a method that follows one of two major schools of thought: the Alpha and R+, which refers to Positive Reinforcement. The Alpha method is closely associated with Pack Theory, Dominance, and Aversive based training.

I started as an Alpha trainer. I used a lot of hard scruff corrections, touch corrections, and alpha rolls. These techniques work very well when applied with the right energy. But most dog owners do not want to take a physical approach, which often means that they perform these techniques with the wrong energy. They are either hesitant because they don't want to do things this way, or they wait until they've become frustrated and perform the techniques with anger. Neither one of those energies work; the risk being that the dog will comply out of fear, instead of trust and respect.

The other standard option is R+, a mainly applied science based method that uses operant conditioning and food rewards. I switched to more of an R+ style within a year of opening my practice. But eventually, I saw a flaw in using strictly positive reinforcement. It does not allow the dog to deal with experiences that cause anxiety, phobia, or aggression in a way that may yield faster results. This way, there is too much comforting and not enough challenge for the dog. We have to encourage the dog out to come out of its comfort zone, only allowing them back in if the situation becomes too intense. Knowing when to back off and maintain a patient approach is the key.

What About Human Accountability?

What both of these major methodologies lack is the human accountability factor. Everyone can agree that humans bear responsibility in the dog training process. But the focus of traditional trainers and their followers seems to be more on establishing and maintaining a consistency of technique. This is important, of course, but there is more to it. Our state of mind during the process is equally vital, perhaps even more so.

Cesar Milan has made the term "calm assertive" a common phrase in dog training. Many people that worked with trainers prior to me say that they have heard about the relationship between human and dog energy. However, none of those trainers explained enough about it, and no one incorporated human personal growth into the strategy of dog training.

This is what distinguishes the Doggyality Method. First, we keep an open mind when choosing techniques. Second, we learn to control our own behavior so that we may guide our dogs in the most effective manner.

On the other hand, there is very little compromise with Alpha and R+. Both sides can identify the merit of their method, but many practitioners are not willing to concede that some of the other side's techniques have reasonable value. Sounds a little like Congress, right?

Enter the Doggyality method, which takes pieces from both major schools of thought, as it seeks the right tools for success. Then it adds real human accountability.

While it is not my intention to "call out" the practitioners of different methods, I am committed to making things right for the dogs I meet instead of insuring that *I* am always right. All methods have relevance in particular cases. Even the physical aspects of Alpha training have merit. I do not use them with my daily practices, but knowing how to do an effective alpha roll can come in handy on the rare occasion when I need to defend myself.

My hope with the Doggyality Method is to unite the dog training, rescue and volunteer communities. We should be open to what others have to offer and use all the available tools so we can do better for our dogs.

A Trainer's Belligerence

One particular R+ trainer sums up the closed-minded view of many trainers I've found trolling the message boards of the Internet dog world. Unfortunately, too many of these people manifest their philosophies in the real world, too.

> "Yes it's true that both methods will work, but even without pet owners being able to speak "dog" they will generally have better results with positive methods. I was brought up as a positive trainer and it was always explained to me that quite apart from anything else punishment wasn't a good idea

because if the first fairly mild punishment didn't work it had to escalate.

For instance, you smack a dog for doing something "wrong" and if it doesn't work you smack harder the next time. This potentially escalates until you are kicking or beating the dog, eventually getting to a point where you are hurting the dog enough to achieve the desired result. That may be overly dramatic but you get my point. Most pet owners are only prepared to take aversive training so far and therefore it doesn't work. If they start off with positive training but don't carry it through correctly at least they won't have done huge amounts of damage to the dog.

As for pack theory, it simply isn't true that we do disservice to dogs and owners by constantly referring to it. Most pet owners consider pack and pack theory to mean the rubbish they have read about for years, such as going through doors first, removing food from a dog so it knows you are Alpha, etc. We need to stop talking about packs and pack theory when dealing with pet owners."

This is just one trainer's view, but it is representative of many in the field that won't use a technique because of its context in another method.

In the examples of going through a door first and removing a dog's food, both actions are perceived by this trainer as macho and intense. You will respect me! That doesn't have to be the context of these exercises. Removing food is a useful tool in preventing food aggression and resource guarding. Having a dog sit at the door while an owner goes out first is a great way of slowing the dog's exit and keeping a calm state of mind. Running out the door ahead of an owner is not only counter–productive to a relaxed walk. It can also be dangerous if you have to go down any steps led by a pulling dog.

There is also a strong suggestion that a physical reprimand is an automatic for an Alpha trainer. This is misleading, as the Alpha style has shifted over the last several years. A simple touch correction can be a useful tool when used sparingly at appropriate times. It is not the same as hitting a dog. Although the trainer admits to adding an element of drama, the thoughts are pretty clear. There's a bit of truth in every joke, right?

There are other techniques in the Alpha repertoire that I do not practice, like using shock or vibration collars. I don't recommend choke or pinch collars, either. For me and how I do my training these days, touch corrections and alpha rolls are happening quite infrequently.

DOMINANCE IS NOT ABOUT INTENSITY— IT'S ABOUT A RELAXED AND CONFIDENT STATE OF MIND.

The Beauty of Blocking

Blocking, however, is a core technique in the Doggyality method. It is a mainly Alpha technique, which I rely on heavily.

Essentially, blocking means that we step in front of a dog to block its movement. We also block to shift a dog's state of mind and redirect its focus back to us. Dogs use blocking as communication. It could be to claim something like a bone. It can also be used to direct movement, like herding.

The main idea of blocking is getting into personal space. Remember the "close talker" from *Seinfeld*? It's uncomfortable to be in that proximity and usually causes a retreating movement. We use blocking because dogs understand it.

Body blocking is considered to be a controversial technique because many R+ trainers will not use it, as they feel it's restrictive. I agree that it is, but I do not consider its restrictions an automatic negative.

In fact, what if we changed the word "restrictions" to "boundaries?" Blocking is performed for guidance, and it's one of the purest forms of communication for a dog. It replaces the word "no" and maintains a partnership aspect of the interaction instead of a mastery context. Blocking is performed with a relaxed state of mind, in contrast with intensity, which only makes it difficult to establish trust.

This is the most important piece of the puzzle. With the Doggyality Method, we want to guide our dogs on the basis of trust and respect, not fear.

Like blocking, putting a dog in a crate is an action that can have multiple meanings. Let's say a dog is displaying unwanted behavior. We grab them and force them into the crate while saying "bad dog" in a hostile tone.

That's punishment.

We could also calmly guide them to the crate, say nothing and close the crate door. That is a time out—same action with two different meanings.

Everything depends on human energy during an interaction. But as good as this sounds in theory, it does not work without understanding and applying the cognitive process. We must do that in a context of personal growth. We will explore both in Part One.

A Client's Testimonial

Throughout this book, you will find first-person accounts from several satisfied clients. Over the years, I am happy to report that I have not only helped many humans and dogs to coexist more peacefully; I have also developed many tremendous friendships with both two–legged and four–legged creatures. Naturally, not everyone is as enthusiastic as I am about personal development creating great relationships with their dogs, but I can safely say I have never had a client that gave an honest effort tell me it doesn't work. In the spirit of transparency, if I had any disgruntled dog owners that were not happy with me and/or my work, I would let you know because we could all learn from my mistakes.

With all of this in mind, let me introduce you to Wendy Kaplan of Ft. Lauderdale—in her own words—whose well–informed perspective should be instructive for anyone curious about the Doggyality Method.

Dogs According to Wendy Kaplan

The thing about The Doggyality Method is that you think you are just training your dog when in fact, you are learning to think differently. For me, Larry himself became a lesson in checking my instincts and engaging the cognitive process.

I work in animal welfare and have access to several great trainers and behaviorists. When I met Larry, I was confused. What did this over–confident, longhaired guy who used words like "submission" and "control"—words that didn't resonate with my positive–only philosophy— think he was going to do so differently?

I'd like to say that the answer is "train my dog," but to only say that would be short changing everything about Larry. From the moment he walked in the door and started interacting with my excessively high anxiety little dog, Shay, Larry challenged every assumption I had.

For example, when he talked about "blocking," I cringed at the word and was ready to kick him out the second he hurt my dog. But what I witnessed was a man who used his body and his presence to tell my nervous little guy, "It's alright, dude; I got this."

In fact, I think Larry used those exact words.

In that moment, I stopped reacting and, instead, relaxed, opening myself up to learning something new. Clearly coddling my poor, little abused rescue dog wasn't enough, or I wouldn't have needed Larry. What he showed me was that, by not reacting and consciously thinking through what I really wanted from my dog, I was able to project the confidence he needed from me. I was able to embody the "I got this" energy that allows my dog to relax.

The effect this has had on my dog and his behavior is amazing. And the shift it has created in me has been quite a nice surprise. Turns out, while I thought I was learning to train my dog, the cognitive process snuck into my own head and my actions. Now, whether I am dealing with dogs or with humans, I try to stop myself from jumping to judgment and impulsively reacting. Instead, I try to stop, breathe, work to understand (which with humans often means asking clarifying questions), and then act accordingly. The result is happier relationships—with colleagues, friends, and of course with my best little buddy.

Finding the Trainer in Each of Us

My colleagues would agree that most dog trainers have special abilities. We can connect with dogs and bond quickly. Teaching our clients techniques is obviously a large part of the training process. But how can we teach them to harness the purity of energy towards dogs that comes naturally to most industry professionals? The answer can be found in the cognitive process and within the realms of personal growth.

Part One:
The Cognitive Process

The Cognitive Process

cognitive [kóg–ni–tiv]: of, relating to, or involving conscious mental activities (such as thinking, understanding, learning, and remembering).

THE COGNITIVE PROCESS applies to both dog and human. For a dog, it's accepting guidance into making more appropriate decisions about their behavior. By relying too heavily on operant conditioning, the dog only learns to behave per cues.

For example, you could have a perfect "leave it" command. The dog approaches an object that is off limits. You say, "leave it," and the dog calmly turns away from the object. That's great, but wouldn't it be better if the dog learned to ignore the object by its own decision instead of being prompted?

Doggyality encourages a thought process for dogs. For specific behaviors, it can help produce better results. Overall, the dog feels more relaxed because the thought process releases pent up mental energy.

The cognitive process I have developed goes far beyond dog training. It incorporates some of the nuances and quirks of my life and that's why I call what I do cognitive training for dogs *and* humans.

When we are cognitive in our thought process, we make better decisions because we're less emotional. We're using everything we have to our advantage—our physiology, our psychology, body mechanics and strategy—everything, in fact, that is available. When we embrace this cognitive style of life, we are present. You may recognize this concept as mindfulness. We are living in the moment, but when we learn from the past, more positive mental impressions can be made. This process will improve the day–to–day quality of your activities. It might not make you rich. It might not make you famous. But it will improve the quality of your life. I am very comfortable saying that if you embrace this process, you will find that life can often be a lot easier than we make it otherwise.

Consider the everyday routines of people and dogs.

People with sedentary jobs are usually tired at the end of the day because they have spent a great deal of mental energy. They can get a little stubborn and cranky. For a dog, it's not terribly different. Barking, digging, chewing, anxiety and willful disobedience can all be caused by pent up mental energy. By using a blocking technique, we make mental impressions that the object or space we are blocking belongs to us. With voluntary compliance, the dog is telling you that he reads you loud and clear.

We can do all of this successfully and calmly without using our voices as dog language is primarily nonverbal. This is where the human part of the cognitive process comes in. We're the ones who are controlling these exercises so it is essential that we set them up for success. Start small, and build a rapport. Increase the difficulty of the exercises as progress is made.

For a blocking exercise, we have a much better chance of success if we start with blocking an object in the corner of a room. That means we only have to block at a 90–degree angle versus what we must do in a 360–degree space, such as you would find if you chose to do blocking in the center of a room. I also recommend starting with a lower value object, so the compliance would be easier to achieve at first. If you try to claim a juicy piece of steak in the first attempt, the pursuit will be too heavy to block. We can work up to more valuable objects.

Identifying the goal and establishing the right procedure is the first step. We must practice regularly, both for the dog to learn and for us to gain familiarity with the technique. We have to be consistent without the actions becoming mundane, so we must be cognitive of the details as we perform the exercises. Implementing the cognitive process into the Doggyality method provides faster and longer lasting results with everything from puppy training to behavioral disorders.

My Learning Curve with Dude

Once upon a time, I started my day off with a flat tire on the way to work. It was pouring rain and I was getting filthy dirty trying to change it, and I realized that this whole mess was also going to cost me the expense of buying a new tire.

Years ago, this would have made me unreasonably angry and completely ruined my day. Things happen all the time which are out of our control. All we can do is control our response. I wanted to be able to say that despite the cruel adversity I was facing, I could be proud of my behavior that day, not disappointed in my reaction to an unfortunate event. So I got it together, put the temporary tire on and drove to the service station. As I waited for the tire to be replaced I was totally relaxed. I believed that something good would come out of this.

On my way back, I spotted a dog, soaking wet, hereafter referred to as Dude. He was walking the centerline of Route 1, south of Route 30 in Lower Merion outside Philadelphia. This is a very busy stretch of road where cars frequently travel upwards of 45 mph. I pulled into the first street possible and went after him. I was deliberate but relaxed. Without any hesitation, I herded him off the street. Dude let me approach him and I looped a slip lead and led him back across the street to my car. I had a crate and training supplies so I went to lift him into the car. Dude growled. It was simple communication, like, "I'm not comfortable with what you are doing." He didn't turn his head back or snap at me. I put him down, and in the interest of safety, I muzzled him. He still wasn't happy about me lifting him but at least he couldn't bite me.

Dude did not have a collar or identification so the first thing I did was get him scanned for a microchip, which was negative. I took him home, dried him up a bit, and gave him food and water. I still had to deal with my responsibilities for the day so I put him in a crate in the ventilated garage. I had to assume at that point that he was not properly vaccinated and therefore kept him in quarantine. Later that day, I examined him more closely. I could see from his body language that he was comfortable around me. He let me touch his tail, his face, around the eyes, ears, paws, and pads with no resistance. Dude ate from my hand and with my hand in his bowl and he had no reaction to me taking away his bowl in the middle of his meal. He let me put my hand in his mouth. I noticed that his teeth on the right side were nubbed down just about to the gums. When I had first spotted him, I thought he had a collar, which turned out to be a rusty chain wrapped twice around his neck. My guess is that he chewed his way out of whatever he was tied to. Dude was underweight and his skin was irritated on the top of his neck from the chain. I later saw comments on a message board that he had been roaming around the area for several weeks.

I had to have Dude vaccinated before he could interact with my dogs and other humans. He got several long walks each day, nutritious food, clean water, and some supervised time to hang out in the yard. The rest of the time he was confined to a crate or a very small area.

To us humans, this almost sounds like the life of a prisoner. For a dog, this is structure. Dude was getting everything he needed to feel secure. I didn't feel bad about how much time he was restricted because at the time, he was still an unstable, stray dog.

Safety is the primary concern in a situation like this. Dude was not ready for heavy interactions. He didn't have any problem with his confinement. He never barked or showed resistance about his restrictions. He would whine for fifteen or twenty seconds in the crate, and then he would settle and relax.

I have taken some criticism on social networks and message boards about my seemingly unemotional nature towards Dude. I also drew criticism for not making enough effort to look for an owner, and the fact that he was crated for a majority of his time. When I first saw Dude, I was so excited about the thought of returning him to a grateful owner. But the condition in which I found him was outright neglectful and I knew the owners wouldn't claim him. I also knew they didn't deserve to have him back. Nonetheless, I did follow the proper legal procedures to see if someone had claimed him.

Believe me, I would have loved to have the opportunity to "chat" with the owner. Animal control would have been right next to me, issuing half a dozen citations for abuse and neglect. But I was non-confrontational with my responses online, assuring people that Dude's best interests were in my heart. Most people could see that and were very supportive. I received many comments and notes commending me on my efforts with Dude. It was inspirational and gave me an amazing feeling.

Dude improved each day. He learned to walk on a leash and earned more time to interact with people and other dogs. His gentle nature showed, as he was interested and polite during his greetings on our walks. Dude accepted every place I took him and every direction I gave.

When we get dogs as companions we enjoy providing affection and they enjoy receiving it. This reward should be associated with a relaxed state of mind. Dude has attained more security by how I've treated him as a dog. That means putting some of my human needs or desires on the shelf in the interest of what is best for Dude.

I sometimes let him work out his problems on his own. I see moments of insecurity here and there, but they are all reasonable under the circumstances. For example, Dude does not seem to like thunderstorms. He becomes clearly unsettled when they swoop in. But when they do occur, I do not pay any attention to him because I don't want to validate the unstable behavior. Instead, I allow him to settle on his own, which he does in less than 15 minutes.

The time to validate his behavior is when he is very relaxed. It's difficult for us not to humanize our dogs because we love them so much. But please remember that they are dogs, and they need trust and leadership to work through their problems.

Dude's case is an outstanding example of the cognitive process from start to finish. There were many occasions for reactionary behavior during those two weeks, both for Dude and for me. A flat tire in a pouring rainstorm is reason enough for a little emotion. Then, I thought I had found someone's lost pet, only to realize that he was a victim of neglect and now my responsibility. If I fed those emotions, it would have been an injustice to the dog. But by keeping my thought process going and staying in the moment with a clear head, I removed the emotion, made good decisions and helped a dog in need. Dude was adopted locally and I still visit him from time to time.

Strategies for Success

We all have goals for our dog. Some of us simply want a well–behaved companion. Others want to take things to a higher level, such as therapy dog certification. Whatever your goals are, they must be identified up front. Procedures must be selected to achieve those goals, and the proper methods must be identified so that they can be implemented.

The details of these procedures are the keys to success. Performing training interactions on a routine, mundane basis will provide inconsistent results and more than likely frustrate the owner. Set up for success by paying attention to detail and following a strategy. Understand why certain things work. For example, most luring hand signals are designed to utilize body mechanics so the dog almost falls into the position we request.

The Stay Command

An example of setting up for success with an individual exercise is the stay command. I use a number system that represents the steps we take away from the dog and the count of pause before returning to the dog for a reward.

For example 1 x 1 is one step back, a one–second pause, then return to treat. I encourage doing 1 x 1 and 2 x 2 the first few days to build a lot of success. It's tempting to see how far we can go and how long the dog can hold out, but that is inviting failed attempts. Take a slow and steady approach and things will go a lot smoother.

Conversely, an impulse control exercise would be more successful by starting further away. When we perform stay, we hold onto the treat. With impulse control, an object treat gets placed on the ground that must be ignored. We have reward treats in our hand for successful attempts. If we place the object treat one foot in front of the dog, there's no way he will resist. By placing the object treat about ten feet away it is easier for him to maintain control of the impulse to go get it. Plus, if he has a failed attempt, we have plenty of time to pick up the object treat before he gets to it.

Training Integration

Another way to set up for success is to go about training exercises in an appropriate order. Recall, or coming when called, is usually one of the first things people want to do with a new dog. Recall is obviously one of the most important things we can teach a dog, but that doesn't mean we need to teach it first. Recall is a higher value exercise than other basic commands.

SUCCESS PYRAMID

Setting up for success is important. Start with the easiest exercise and build up from there.

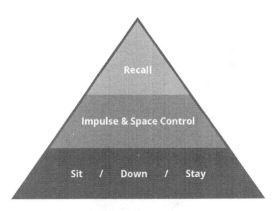

RIGHT WAY

WRONG WAY

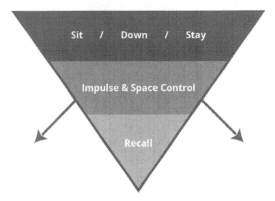

I like to build success with easier items. Bonding and building trust are essential for a good recall and can be earned starting with easier exercises, like sit, down, and stay. It's like building a house; we need the sit, down, and stay as a foundation. Then we can add the first floor and then the second. I think it is much easier to teach a dog to come after they have learned how to stay, rather than vice versa.

Run Away Recall

The cognitive process also questions other uses for commands than the normal circumstances. If a dog gets away from us, our first instinct is to call the dog back. In my experience, a very solid stay command trumps a potentially inconsistent recall command. This is especially the case if the dog has crossed a street. I don't want them running back across it to get to me. I want them to stay and I'll go to them.

Having a full understanding of dogs also makes for better decisions. A lot of dog training ideas and techniques may seem counterintuitive, yet they make perfect sense if we look at them from a dog's perspective. When a dog is loose, and we can't recall them, we think we need to chase and catch them. But this turns it into a game for the dog and they will run further away. Instead, try getting the dog's attention, and then running excitedly in the other direction. This will pique the dog's curiosity and they will more than likely chase you.

I call this Run Away Recall.

Turning Everyday Interactions into Training Exercises

No matter what technique is used, dogs will not be good at their commands without practicing them. A frequent question I get is how long training should be each day. The answer to that question is not unlike many other things in life. You get out of it what you put into it. I generally suggest spreading out exercises throughout the day and evening, rather than trying to schedule 30 to 45 minutes sessions. It is usually unrealistic for many households to block out that kind of time on a daily basis.

That being said, combining daily household activities and training exercises is a great way to set up for success. One of the pitfalls for many dog owners is not following up with training after the initial goals have been accomplished. Many of us become complacent because the dog now knows the behaviors we have encouraged. But without continued practice, many dogs will regress.

I ask people every day what commands their dog knows. They state between three and five commands. Then I ask what commands their dog performs on a consistent basis without reward. That list shortens to one or two. This is because they are not regularly practiced.

So let's look at some household activities which lend themselves to integrating training exercises. Going up and down the stairs is a great one. The dog should wait at the bottom or top of the stairs until we go up or down. This is not about Alpha or who is the boss. This is about having the opportunity to practice a sit or down, then a wait and release. It is also a great way to practice the recall command by using the recall word on the release.

We're combining basic commands, space–control, and impulse control into a meaningful exercise and replacing a previously thoughtless act. We can practice this naturally numerous times during the day. The bonus prize of this exercise is safety, especially in a household with small children, when a dog running up and down the stairs without control can be hazardous. There should be procedures in place to deal with other daily activities, like answering the door and keeping the dog away from human food areas.

Controlling *You* Before Your Dog

It's pretty simple. If we can't control our own behavior, why do we expect our dogs to control theirs? One reason why my clients generally have more success and achieve higher levels of satisfaction with their dogs is because they assume responsibility. It's not entirely about the dog; it's equally about the humans.

During a session, I may say, "A lot of this is about controlling behavior." When I say that, most people look at their dog. I noticed it casually at first, then I began to pay closer attention. By looking at the dog, I infer that they think I'm referring to controlling the dog's behavior. I'm actually talking about us controlling our own human behavior.

The connection between our human energy output and our dog's response to our vibe is constantly relevant, even when it's not involved in a direct interaction with the dog. We have to go beyond focusing on the dog's state of mind and focus as much on our own state of mind, That way, we can control our behavior and energy output.

For example, what happens in your house when you come home from work and greet your dog at the door? Most of us come into our homes and make a big fuss. We love it and our dogs love it. Everybody's happy. Then a guest comes over and the dog jumps on the guest. We tell them not to do that; yet we have validated that behavior day after day by providing affection as we encourage their enthusiastic welcome.

The door is associated with excitement and emotion because we made it like that. The dog begs for food because we cave in and give them some. Then we want them to stay away from the dinner table. Again, we've rewarded them for being in that space.

We like doing these things for our dogs. We like to have those interactions. But those interactions are setting a bad example for how we would actually like the dog to behave. When we contradict our own behaviors, we are also conditioning our dogs to misbehave.

IF WE CAN'T CONTROL OUR OWN BEHAVIOR, WHY DO WE EXPECT OUR DOGS TO CONTROL THEIRS?

Most people don't like the idea of waiting a few minutes to greet their dogs. They usually think it is mean. Dogs won't take offense to it; they'll be just as happy to see you five minutes later as they would at that moment. And during those moments of waiting, the dog learns how to relax in order to receive attention properly. Plus, if we reward them away from the door, we take away the door as "the place to be."

Of course, even those who understand this theory can still be hesitant to practice it. These same people will tell me that they are a dog lover. Now to me, a dog lover is someone who puts their human desires on the shelf and can focus on the needs of their dogs.

Many dogs get very excited during the walk and for several reasons. They react to people and most dogs with excitement. There are some dogs they are selective about, which is common for most dogs. With a proper introduction, things would probably work out well, but leashes add tension. Dogs feel restricted by the leash and get frustrated. The onset of several emotional responses sends out a very excited energy and other dogs will often match that energy. At that point, there is too much excitement to maintain any focus, so it's best to get the dogs relaxed and try again.

Using Non–Verbal Communication

A blocking procedure combined with a loose leash will contain the excitement. Then, you can allow your dog to re–approach starting from a calm place. Restraint causes tension, which fuels more emotion. This is back–end work; meaning, the event has already begun and we are trying to contain it.

The idea is to associate a number scale, say 1 to 10. The dog is at #1 when relaxed in both body and mind. This does not mean the dog has to be lying down. A dog can be at #1 while walking. If the dog's mind is engaged, there is a break in the flow and the energy starts at levels #2 to #3. Most commonly, dogs will start a "look" at the object. Levels #4 to #6 occur when the look becomes a stare. If not controlled quickly, a stare can change to fixation and levels #7 to #8.

When action occurs, we're at level #9 to #10.

Identify what level #1 looks like and establish the baseline energy of your dog. Within a few seconds, the dog has moved through all levels and into action. By stepping in front, we're communicating disapproval of the current action and state of mind.

This is nonverbal communication.

Using voice prompts will only add excitement, not reduce it. The dog doesn't really understand most of the words we're using, anyway. Even the ones that it does know are ineffective because the dog is fixated on something else.

Picture a pro basketball player about to attempt a free throw when the score is tied with two seconds left in game seven of the finals. The arena is going crazy. Fans are screaming and waving their arms behind the basket. The shooter doesn't hear the noise or see the motion. He's locked in on the basket and nothing else matters. His state of mind is at level #10. When a dog is at Level #10, saying No! No! No! at that point has the same meaning as saying Go! Go! Go!

This happens not because of the word, but because of the energy in that exact moment. We are changing our inflection; our movements are erratic, not controlled. Our frustration is making us emotional, and that causes a heightened level of instability for a dog.

The Magic of Distraction

The progression from level #1 to #10 usually happens in a matter of seconds. That's why it seems so hard to control. That's why recognition of the levels is a key tool in helping our dogs through reactive situations. I think most dog owners know the expressions of their own dogs. The look, stare, and fixation expressions are pretty easy to identify. If we don't catch it in time, things escalate quickly. Once we see the look, we must first practice there.

Immediately respond with a distraction.

I choose the word distraction here because there is nothing wrong with a look. A level #2 look is an awareness of the environment. A level #4 stare initiates the reactive stimulus.

Distraction at level #2 can get a dog to recoil back to level #1. Examples are a verbal prompt (including things like a human whistle or snap) and a motion prompt.

In a controlled manner, wave your arms or use your body to block vision. When your dog focuses on you, step into their space, which is asking them to retreat. If leashed, try to use very limited tension and loosen up and much as possible. We're not trying to become intense at this point, because the dog will match our energy.

We need to perform these actions with a stable but relaxed posture and state of mind. Your body will be the restraint. Use it as a physical barrier and reduce leash tension. Our dogs are looking to us for direction. We must show confidence and relaxation to guide them through difficult situations. This requires control of our behavior.

I don't want to control the dog's behavior. I want to control the environment and guide dogs toward the ability to control their own behavior.

The Science of Decision–Making

We make small decisions throughout the day that can affect a lot more than our current, momentary situation. Inevitably, most of these mundane decisions influence our stress levels.

Naturally, they invariably ebb–and–flow throughout the course of any given day, but it's how we handle that rollercoaster that determines our short– and long–term health.

For example, many people share frustration when it comes to being delayed, whether it's in traffic or at the grocery store checkout. It's understandable that we react because these delays usually come at inconvenient times. But they happen—like the weather—and that is out of our control. The only thing we have control over is our behavior. We have a choice about how we deal with delays and inconveniences. If we become frustrated, chances are we will carry that state of mind forward into our next personal and/or business transaction. One stress–filled scenario may lead to another and another, creating some very unwanted, unproductive and anxious momentum, which will more than likely affect the way we deal with our dog, too.

For example, in that grocery store line, we could choose to feed that tension and frustration. Then we rush out to the car and back out of our spot too fast and hit someone. How much time and money will that cost us? In that anxious state of mind, we are inviting more problems that will negatively affect our decision–making ability, costing us more time, not to mention an accident. Texting while driving, anyone? Are you freaking out because you're running late and you're sure the world will end if your schedule gets messed up?

Depending on the severity of a mistake, becoming emotional (for no good reason) may cost a whole lot more than you bargained for. It affects our thought process and increases the chance of poor decision–making. Even if we get through these situations with seemingly no further consequence, the stress factor will add up during the day and take its toll, even affecting the quality of our family time and the downtime we normally enjoy with our dog. By allowing the frustrations of the day to mount, we have expended a lot of mental and physical energy

Breathe.

Luckily, there are options.

Let's go back to that grocery store line. If we have to spend three or four minutes—or God forbid even more—in that situation, then why not make them productive minutes, or better yet, relaxed?

Converting Threat to Opportunity

A client once complained that he had no time for himself. His career and family demands continued to pile high and there was just not any time left over to consider his own wants and needs. He really felt deprived of quality alone time. He then went on to explain that traffic eats away a large chunk of that time and it's become a constant source of frustration.

I asked if he realized that he already had the answer to his problem. I explained that by applying the cognitive process, he could choose to identify the commute as quality alone time, rather than a source of ongoing stress. He could enjoy some good music or an audio book. He could bring a drink and a snack. He might even choose to pay attention to the environments he is driving through and let his mind wander into areas he usually would not entertain.

This brings me to one of my favorite strategic planning tools: ETOP, which stands for Environmental Threat and Opportunity Profile. It is one of the most effective applications of the cognitive process. In simple terms, we survey our environments for potential threats, and then use our thought process to convert these perceived threats into opportunities.

An example would be a restaurant in a small town. Let's say it's the only establishment in town and all the locals go there to eat. You're the owner. On what seems like just another calm and ordinary day, somebody opens a restaurant across the street. It's more than likely that you would perceive that as a threat to your business.

At that point, you must employ a natural thought process and make a crucial choice. You can convert this potential negative threat into a positive opportunity.

> ## THREAT IS FELT WITH EMOTION. OPPORTUNITY IS PURSUED THROUGH A THOUGHT PROCESS.

First, a business with an established customer base may have a tendency to become somewhat complacent. In small towns with one place to eat, this wouldn't be surprising. Competition forces a business to tighten up and perform to its potential. It may even inspire creativity. Your customers will be happier with their experience. You can win new business on the basis of merit, not by default.

Second, the new restaurant owner will be advertising his grand opening and promoting his new business. They will be attempting to bring in people from surrounding areas that may not know about your restaurant. Those people will see your place and become potential new diners the next time they're in town. And your competitor just paid for your next customer.

If more restaurants open, they have the potential to draw more and more people to that area with the intention of dining. It is up to each individual business to achieve customer loyalty. We see this example come to life with car dealerships and gas stations and drive–thru banks. When one establishment takes hold in an area and does well, you can be pretty sure that others of the same ilk will follow.

ETOP in the Extreme

Applying the cognitive process can be a lifesaver. In my case, I learned this through an interaction with a highly aggressive dog. When unwanted behavior becomes a threat to our peaceful environment, our household items, or the safety of a human or another dog, it can also spiral into a source of real despair.

In one particular case I experienced not long ago, the threat to my safety became quite real and I was fortunate to be able to turn a highly dangerous situation into an opportunity for genuine training.

The owners of a large power breed dog asked me to help them with their dog's aggression. Unfortunately, they were less than truthful in our initial phone consultation about their dog's level of aggression. I walked into a situation where the dog literally tried to kill me.

He attacked the instant I walked into the house by jumping up and biting my arm. I was able to fend him off and then move into his space. He jumped up toward my head and I fended him off again, this time with a little more force. This made him to back up nearly all the way across the room. He growled at me. I asked the owners to remain calm. When he growled again, one of the owners screamed at him, which caused the dog to react by running across the room and leaping toward my face. I was able to fend him off again but not before he bit my face and neck. He actually missed my carotid artery by about a centimeter. I took three puncture wounds, and was bleeding from my arm, neck, and face. I remained calm and got the dog into the crate. Only then did the owners share the real situation by revealing their dog's attack history that they had withheld during our original phone consultation.

As some of my friends and family found out about this incident, they asked if it was going to stop me from seeing aggression cases, some of which directly threaten my safety. At first, I thought they had a point, but then I remembered ETOP and how I had integrated those principles in my uncommon encounter with this inherently aggressive dog.

I viewed the interaction as an opportunity to see what I could handle under the worst possible scenario. I can say that I handled it well and that anyone with less than outstanding dog handling skills may have been killed that day. It would have been reasonable to be scared after this incident. In fact, it could have simply ended my dealings with aggression cases.

Instead, I became empowered by handling such an intense situation in a positive manner. This incident also enabled me to refine my screening process and entry procedures for aggression cases. I exercise more caution now, and have the owners crate or tether an aggressive dog before I enter their house. This allows me to safely interact with the dog and avoid flare ups. Once I connect with the dog and understand the source of their behavior, I can begin treating them.

Threat is felt with emotion. Opportunity is pursued with a logical thought process. In my case, turning a threat into an opportunity allowed me to move forward and keep working with difficult cases that really need my help.

Alicia Harantschuk's Passion for Pet Therapy
(According to Alicia)

With a mini Dachshund with guarding issues and an anxious pit mix, I needed help preparing my dogs for the world of pet therapy. I did some research over the phone here in Pennsylvania, and right from the start I had a really good feeling about Larry. I arranged our first session.

Olivia Lee Longbottom, our mini Dachshund, is nine pounds and fearless with some resource guarding issues when it comes to food, certain toys and me. Let's not skip over the fact that she also wanted to be the alpha dog in our house. I had my own work to do establishing leadership in the house. In addition to the "No, Yes, No" (now referred to as "Your Time, Our Time") game, I had to claim objects that were mine until I said she could have them, with the option for me to reclaim them at any time.

Larry's approach offered blocking techniques, obedience exercises and more.

When we adopted Miss Vegas, our pocket pitty, we were a little nervous how the two dogs would get along. Vegas was extremely obedient, submissive and loved learning new things. Larry's guidance made for a smooth integration. We thought Vegas would make a great therapy dog; however, as she transitioned from the puppy stage, she became nervous and anxious from things like loud noises and new objects.

I signed her up for a therapy dog test and worried about how she would handle the exposure to noise, as well as interacting with crutches and wheelchairs. I called on Larry again. Like previous sessions, his approach was spot on. The back and forth style of desensitizing Vegas to the noise was the right amount of challenge without pushing it too far.

I will never forget Larry skipping around my yard with a cooking pot lid, dropping it and letting it roll around. Vegas was nervous at first but by the end of the session she was much less stressed and far more accepting. The best part was, she passed the therapy test with flying colors.

It's important to point out that my two dogs have totally different "doggyalities."

The way Larry combines Alpha and R+ methods is pure genius and works for all types of issues or unwanted behaviors. His approach is never harmful or inhumane to the dog. He never puts you on a path where the dog behaves only because they are afraid of the consequences.

Larry also factors in the humans in a dog's life. Knowing that dogs feel and react to our energy and addressing how we can better communicate with our dogs is a key component of his work. We need to monitor our posture and tone of voice as well as how much affection we give our dogs, and when.

Fast forward three years. Olivia will gladly sit on anyone's lap or accept affection from a patient while I hold her. When I ask her to get on her bed, she knows that she needs to stay until I release her. I can put my hand in her food bowl at any time without issue.

As for Vegas, she's still afraid of thunder but no longer shuts down during a storm. She's gained much needed confidence and earned her Champion Trick Dog title.

Olivia and Vegas have collectively completed 183 therapy visits since being certified in September 2013. I would not have been able to accomplish so much if it weren't for the foundational work I did with Larry. My opinion of Larry has not changed and my respect for his abilities has never been greater.

But something else has changed dramatically: the relationship with my dogs. At 44 years old and after growing up with animals my entire life, I never thought owning a dog could be like this and I never thought a dog trainer could help me become a better person. In fact, because of Olivia I got involved with volunteering and helping others, which has had the most amazing impact on my life. I resigned from my job of 15 years to go with a start up and had it written into my contract that I would have certain flexibility in my schedule allowing time for my volunteer work. This has made me a better person and I will be forever grateful to Olivia—and Larry—for that.

Reflex Versus Thought Process

Have you ever been stopped at a red light, and when the light turned green, you just took off? Of course, we do that all the time. Have you ever driven down the road about 50 yards and then wondered if the light did in fact turn green? We don't remember. Sometimes, we go to work or to the grocery store and wonder how we even got there. (And that's without any wine.)

This is because we are behaving from our purely reflexive nature without the benefit of using our God–given ability to process thought. It kind of redefines the concept of being absent minded. In fact, our minds are not absent. We just forget to use them!

THE DOG THAT THINKS
WILL WAIT FOR CUES—
NOT ANTICIPATE THEM.

When we only want dogs to follow our commands, we produce reflexed behavior. One of the drawbacks to reflexed behavior is that several commands can be taught in succession.

At first, we teach a dog to lay down from a sitting position. I usually prefer to switch them over to down from a standing position as soon as possible to avoid the guesswork of what's next. When we train in succession, the dog may start to assume the next command instead of waiting for the cue.

Another common example of this is when we say, "Sit." The dog sits and then automatically tries to give paw. We didn't ask for it; they just assume it comes next because they have been conditioned to think that way through repetition.

The dog that thinks will wait for cues—not anticipate

them. Relying on reflex only limits the potential of our dogs. Engaging the thought process makes mental impressions of desired behavior. With a voluntary compliance, the dog is more likely to repeat the desired behavior by decision. This will be discussed in more detail in Part Two.

Cause and Effect Versus Logic and Reason

Redirection is a very common technique used by many dog trainers. If a dog is mouthy or nipping, we can generally assume that they want to play or chew. Since chewing is reasonable behavior for a dog, especially puppies, we encourage it. Of course our hand or arm is not an appropriate chew toy, so we redirect to an acceptable item for chewing.

This makes perfect sense—for a human—because we have better logic and reason.

For a dog, who uses cause and effect, this is interpreted as follows:

"Nip, get a toy. Nip, get a toy. Nip, get a toy."

And we wonder why they keep nipping us!

The concept of redirection is valid and useful, but I think it needs an adjustment. We need to respond to the nip so the association is a consequence, not a reward. The consequence can be as simple as a withdrawal of affection, as in just a small step back. If the dog responds with voluntary compliance, we can provide affection again. The repetition of this teaches the dog that affection is associated with compliance, not nipping.

Can you say "Cognitive Thinking?"

"Stay" Is a State of Mind

Let's go back to the stay command. Most people consider stay to be a body position. The dog is in the spot where we asked him to be and he remains there until we release him. A seemingly successful exercise, but is position all that matters? I don't believe so.

Stay should be a feeling, not a body position.

My cousin Jeff in Israel said that to me several years ago. It resonated right away. State of mind is just as important as the body position. We discussed the techniques for teaching stay, and we both found it strange that stay is taught to puppies with a release.

In my experience, about half the people questioned responded that stay and release was how they thought it should be done. This is just as it sounds. The dog stays until we release. Then he runs to us and gets a treat.

The problem here is that the dog is being rewarded for the act of coming, not for the act of staying. Since the reward part is more valuable to the dog, he remains with intense anticipation, like a runner in the starting blocks waiting for the gun to go off.

This is not the state of mind we should be looking to encourage. When the dog is in the stay position, a relaxed state of mind is more beneficial. Therefore, we should be returning back to the dog to provide the reward. This way, he learns to wait patiently. The dog is back on its heels, so to speak, not leaning forward in anticipation.

Promoting better focus transfers to all situations of unwanted behaviors. When the thought process part of the brain is engaged, the emotional part shuts down. This is a physiological attribute that dogs and humans share. We've always been told not to make decisions when we are upset, as they tend to yield poor outcomes. When we can shift from an emotional response to a thought process, we make better decisions. This lends particular value in impulse–control. This is not only relevant to us. The same theory applies to our dogs.

What If We Were More Like Dogs?

As humans, we can learn quite a bit from living life more like a dog. First of all, they don't have grudges. They aren't spiteful. They don't carry things over. They just live in the present. Wherever they are, that's the place to be. For the most part, that's the life of a dog.

Of course I am talking about a stable dog. I am not referring to a dog that has a behavior disorder of some sort. But if you have a stable dog, he or she is just happy. And when a dog isn't happy, it doesn't complain.

We humans have a lot of outlets for venting and ranting—whatever term you may choose for expressing our feelings. Doing so in the moment can be a good thing as long as it's done in a positive way. To become stuck in the moment reflecting in a negative manner doesn't really make it. It just won't get you through to a positive place.

Let's imagine your family goes outside to the backyard where there are two sheds. You go inside one shed and your dog goes into the other. The doors to the sheds are closed and locked. Your family returns to the house to watch TV or play a board game. An hour later, they come back outside and open the doors of the sheds.

Inside Shed #1 they discover one angry human. Inside Shed #2 they find one happy dog.

The dog greets everyone happily and doesn't care that it's just been locked in the shed all alone for an hour. But you, on the other hand, are not a happy camper.

This scenario clearly demonstrates what it means to live the moment. Wherever you are, that's the place to be. Of course, no one wants to be locked in a shed for an hour. But is it going to kill us? No. Is it going to harm us in any way? No. All it's going to do is force us to look at the world in a different way. We could simply accept it and see it as a perfect opportunity. Instead of being angry and aggravated with the person who just locked us in the shed for an hour, we could thank them for giving us an hour of peace and quiet to think about life and reflect. The more we engage this kind of thought process, the more empowered we become.

Homer's Odyssey

One of my clients this year experienced something with her yellow lab that is worth sharing. I think it illustrates a lot about acceptance and resilience—two lessons we humans can certainly learn from our dogs. I'll leave it to Homer's human to tell the story.

On February 18th of this year, Homer woke up with a lame, left front leg. He wouldn't put any weight on it. We thought it might be Lyme disease since we'd had another dog present that way in the past. I took him to the local vet that morning. She thought that maybe Homer had a pulled muscle and she wasn't terribly concerned. But we thought it was just too odd since he hadn't really done any activity the previous day that would have pulled or sprained a muscle.

The vet offered to do an X–ray just to make sure there wasn't anything else going on and it revealed a tumor on his ulna. Then she took pictures of his spine area and an ultrasound of his bladder area to make sure there was no spread, which there wasn't. Homer's basic blood work was also good. The vet said it was probably osteosarcoma and suggested that we see a specialist to get the pathology straight.

A week later, we met the oncologist and because of where the tumor was located, they had to do an open biopsy, which meant a surgery. They performed it that day and we picked Homer up the next morning.

That was his first surgery. He was given a few stitches and had to wear the "cone of shame" for 10 days. Almost two weeks later, the test results confirmed that it was an osteosarcoma. We discussed doing an ulnectomy (removing just the ulna—the forearm bone), but were told that dogs do much better with an amputation than with partial bone removal, which could risk leaving him with a chronically painful limb.

We chose amputation. I took Homer in on March 6th and he stayed over two nights before we could bring him home.

At first, he was in pretty significant pain. He had a hard time getting comfortable because he couldn't roll on his back or on his side due to the stitches, which had to stay in for ten days. He has been tired but it's hard to tell whether it's the meds, the chemo or the exhaustion of hopping around on three legs.

For us, the remarkable thing has been that he doesn't seem to realize that he's got different capabilities now. He was licking at the dishes in the dishwasher even when he was wearing the stupid cone that blocked his ability to do so. He's desperate to go on walks and always tries to walk farther than he can. We had to pick him up in the car when we let him go too far. When he's tired, he still whines to go upstairs and go to bed, even though he doesn't know how to get down the stairs yet. I have to carry him!

Homer returned to counter surfing last week and also hopped into the groomer's truck as well as onto the groomer's table. At this point, less than a month post–surgery and one chemo treatment later, he's up to walking from our house around the block and up another long street until we circle back home. We do this twice a day. We're going to be working on stairs very soon so that he can return to sleeping upstairs.

What I've Learned from Dogs

I visited Homer on March 19th and all he wanted to do was go for a walk. He was so happy to see me, and came hopping over to greet me as he always did before the surgery. This was one month and one day after he was diagnosed, and just 13 days post–op. If it had been me on the operating table, I would probably still be clicking the morphine button and feeling sorry for myself about losing a limb. Homer had no regard for his own plight. He was just a happy dog enjoying another day of life.

Homer reminded me of why I love working so much with dogs. They have made me a better person in so many ways. Here are 10 things I've learned from dogs:

1. To live life in the present.
2. To love more unconditionally.
3. To not practice spiteful behavior or hold grudges.
4. To be more patient and compassionate.
5. To put the needs of others above my own desires.
6. To feel a sense of reward for pleasing others.
7. To suffer silently, without always ranting to friends, family, and on social media.

     Sometimes we feel a release of tension from a good rant, and on occasion, it can be constructive. But mostly, it releases negative energy and fuels more of the same. Imagine not even feeling the need to rant. We control what we can and let go of the rest.
8. To not be self–conscious.
9. To live without constant judgment—of myself and others.
10. To not fear death.

I often work seven days a week. Every day I don't help a dog, I feel like I'm denying myself pleasure. (Then again, I do enjoy the occasional round of golf.)

Most of all, I've learned that when you want to feel good about yourself, do something for somebody else. Maybe we should be more like dogs…

Part Two:
Puppies, Rescues
and Special Needs

GPS: Guide Pooch Straight

We live in an age of ever–advancing technology; and for those of us who rely on a GPS to navigate our way through an unfamiliar world, step–by–step instructions are invaluable. So just as we use this system to guide ourselves, we can also operate as our dogs' GPS. We can show them step–by–step instructions on how to reach their destination, which is a goal for each interaction.

By understanding how to get through everyday household situations, dogs can have a happy and well–adjusted life. Sure, they will make wrong turns on occasion—so it is up to us to re–route them.

Sound familiar? "What's wrong with Google maps? I can't find my destination!"

Since I encourage the practice of nonverbal communication using a minimal amount of voice guidance, dogs will learn how to reach their destination if and when we guide them the same way every time.

When someone asks me if I know where I'm going, I always say that I'll just follow my GPS. Most people I know say the same thing. We trust that this technology knows the way better than we do. Wouldn't it be nice to provide your dog with the same regularity and confidence by becoming their steady and reliable GPS?

Dogs are a big part of our world and their security depends on our guidance. It's vital that we establish that foundation as we train them to live well and prosper.

We can begin by teaching them basic commands and other desired behaviors.

Teaching Basic Commands: Physical Prompting, Luring, Behavior Capture

Physical Prompting: This occurs when we assist the dog's body into our desired position. Physical prompting should be performed in a gentle manner. The goal is not to force; it's to guide. Sometimes, dogs have trouble on a floor and won't do "Down" because they slip or don't feel secure in their footing. In that case, we would secure their back end in the sit position and gently guide their front paws into the down position. This approach is meant as a last resort. Never attempt physical prompting if you suspect your dog may have an injury, has arthritis, dysplasia or some other ailment, or if it causes physical discomfort.

Luring: This is the most common technique to teach the basics and beyond. It's also the most self–explanatory. Use a food reward to lure the dog into the desired place or position and release the treat at the exact point of compliance.

Behavior Capture: This is a lesser–utilized technique but it is still valuable. Many trainers refer to it as shaping. Sometimes, dogs do not follow luring, especially if they are not food motivated. Anxiety or physical limitations can take physical prompting out of the equation. With behavior capture we reinforce a command word or validate behavior that was random. In other words, we didn't ask for it. So if a dog walks around for a moment and then lies down, we could say "good down" just as their belly hits the floor.

Word to Action Versus Action to Word

I really like behavior capture because it associates a word to an action, instead of associating an action to a word. There is a big difference between those two phrases. The dog is already performing the action on his own, so all we are doing is labeling it naturally. The other way around, we are saying a word and hoping to get the dog to learn the action and word at the same time. That means we have to use a prompt—physical or verbal—to get the behavior we desire.

We can also use behavior capture as a supplement to luring, just to make the association more meaningful.

The drawback to behavior capture is that it has to happen naturally and we're not always ready to validate it. If we haven't set up the exercise, we don't get as much opportunity for repetition.

A fun way to use behavior capture is using your dog's natural tendencies to teach them cool tricks. After enough repetition, it can imprint.

Hobie is a buddy of mine that excels at fetch. He always brings it back and always drops it. Sometimes, Hobie gets excited and "throws" the ball instead of dropping it. I noticed this a few times and started labeling that action as "throw," calling it out each time he did a throw instead of a drop.

The mental impression was made. Now we play a fun game where he throws the ball and I try to kick it from the air. Quite honestly, that ball gets way too slimy to keep picking it up with my hand! I'm glad Hobie has learned how to throw it.

And, by the way, he can also chase it down and make a Willie Mays style basket catch. It's awesome.

Remember: behavior capture requires natural events and precise timing.

Three Forms of Compliance

According to Merriam–Webster's dictionary, "compliance" is defined as "the act or process of doing what you have been asked or ordered to do." In a dog's world, or at least the one I occupy, compliance is a feeling, not a body position. This may be better understood if we think back to the benefits of cognitive thinking. It makes a lot of sense when it comes to instilling compliance.

Whether your dog is a puppy, a rescue or one with special needs, compliance is a necessary tool.

Forced Compliance: This is accomplished by putting the dog on its side or back using a physical maneuver. This is commonly referred to as an Alpha Roll. It can be a very effective technique, though it has to be delivered with an even–keeled energy. Most people have a problem with this because their emotions get in the way. When owners feel bad that they are using a physical technique, they are hesitant. More often, however, they have let the dog frustrate them and the technique is subsequently performed with frustration. Neither will be effective. The dog has to understand that you mean business, but also that you are confident and trustworthy. Though it is rare that I need to use a forced compliance these days, it's good to know how to physically control a dog in case of an emergency situation.

Commanded Compliance: This is a process of using the basic command structure to control the dog's movements. When we teach basic commands, we use operant conditioning. We get a conditioned response from a repeated process. Though commands are necessary, and quite useful in many situations, learning commands doesn't make your dog an obedient dog. And it certainly doesn't mean you have a meaningful relationship.

Voluntary Compliance: The most valuable compliance occurs on a voluntary basis. We use the blocking technique to control the dog's movement and create space inhibition. Dogs react to blocking in different ways. Many dogs will bark and become emotional based on an insecurity of not having freedom of movement. In that case, stay calm. It's better that they get a little frustrated instead of us. Plus, they are using physical energy and we are not. Others dogs will practice avoidance and run away on the same basis. At these points, we must keep our movements deliberate and our minds and bodies relaxed. The dog is looking to us to see how to act.

If we try to match a dog's energy, we will lose.

Instead, we invite the dog to match our stable energy.

compliance is a feeling, not a body position

If we can stay patient and see the exercise through, we show the dog a leadership quality that they crave. And during that time, they are using the cognitive process to figure it out. This will release pent-up mental energy, and allows the dog's mind to relax. Once the mind is relaxed, the body follows, and the dog is receptive to our instructions.

Another benefit of this method is that ultimately the dog chose to perform the proper behavior. It was a conscientious decision, not a conditioned response, so the dog is more likely to repeat the behavior. By validating the voluntary compliance, we make mental impressions of proper behavior.

When we move on to more advanced procedures like answering the door, the benefits of voluntary compliance are clear. The doorbell rings, and if your dogs are anything like mine, they will charge the door. This is a very natural behavior for a dog. I for one do not discourage it because it serves as an excellent deterrent from burglary. Though most of the time dogs are just excited to see some of their favorite visitors, we should be able to control the reaction. When they are at the door, we step in front of them and use blocking to clear them from the door area.

It's best to designate a spot or "place" for the dog to wait for the guest to enter. Once directed to their place, we wait for voluntary compliance. This will help them remain calm, and then they get to greet the guest.

Most dogs will not progress to the point where the doorbell rings and they go directly to their place, but it does happen. Many people ask me if a food reward is appropriate. It is not. Food rewards are not recommended during exercises that use voluntary compliance. The reason for this is that it adds a stimulus just after the point of relaxation. If we're still imprinting, stimulus causes emotion, which nulls the thought process. Then no mental impression is made.

Mental Impressions

These are the key to long–term success. The association they have with a word or interaction can make a big difference on their state of mind during the event. We have mental impressions of favorite people, foods, or vacation destinations. We don't have to be in our paradise, eating those foods, or speaking to those people. We can just think of them and we feel good.

The food reward creates a positive mental impression of the command word. Clients often ask about verbal praise. While it is excellent to match the command word to the desired behavior, it can also be a stimulus. Temper your reward tones to keep the dog's focus during initial training exercises.

Conditioning Behavior Through Cause and Effect

All interactions with a dog require consistency. It's not just how often we make associations, but that we do them the same way every time. And that does not only apply to training interactions. All interactions count. The cause and effect style of dog learning means that they are constantly gathering information from all interactions. That means we have to keep things very consistent and make sure that those interactions are communicating what we want.

Behavior capture is a great way to communicate during a general interaction. Making the mental impressions helps your dog in other situations because they can generalize it. For example, when I'm with Shamus and it's quiet time, I am petting him, and he's getting a lot of affection. During a calm and relaxed time like this, he is receptive. I say the same things to him all the time.

"You're my buddy; you're my buddy boy," things like that.

I always keep the word "buddy" in there, so to him, that word will always be associated with something positive. I also use that whenever I need to introduce him to a new dog. When I show him the dog, but before he gets to greet, I always use the word buddy.

I say, "Shamus, this is your buddy! Look! This is your buddy, Loki.

I repeat the word buddy before saying the name of the new dog. Using the word buddy on a consistent basis causes a positive mental impression to kick in. Therefore, Shamus's first experience with *seeing* the dog—not even meeting the dog yet—just seeing the dog, puts him in a positive state of mind. There is little opportunity for him to go any other way. Of course, if it's a very unstable dog, then there could be some reactions no matter what positive triggers I use. That's why they have to see each other before they meet. They have to be in close proximity without showing signs of excitement, anxiety, phobia or aggression.

Case Study: Shamus Meets a New Dog

When Shamus meets a dog for the first in my house, he's in a room with glass panels on the door so he can see right through. When I bring the new dog into the house, Shamus stays in that room, watching as we walk in.

Cassie, my other personal dog, is in the next room over, also with a glass door, so she can see into Shamus' room as well as out into the hallway where I'm bringing in the new dog.

Shamus is more polite than Cassie when it comes to greeting new dogs. Cassie is very dominant and territorial and she likes to let a new dog know that right away. I've learned to have her greet second after Shamus because that gives us all a better chance of success. Greeting both at one time can be overwhelming for a new dog; it will create too much excitement, so I don't allow that.

I will walk in and Shamus will look and I will immediately watch him. I don't look at the dog that I am bringing in; I look at Shamus. I know him so well by now that his reactions and body language will tell me what he's thinking about the other dog. If the energy is good, then I will open the door and let him come in to greet the other dog. I will generally turn the other dog at that point, and hold the dog in a position where Shamus can sniff his back side. If there is no reaction, then I will turn Shamus around and let the other dog sniff Shamus.

That's a manual procedure that you would follow at any meet–and–greet process. And even before that, there's a proximity drill. While there are proximity drills specifically for doing outside, the first proximity drill I use is Shamus looking, not interacting; just looking through the glass. Keeping him there in a stable state is important to the meet–and–greet process.

It's important to show the other dog that there's nothing to worry about. I count on Shamus for that. I'm starting off at Level #1 — zero intensity. For you golfers, we're at even par. From there, I will gauge Shamus's reaction and see what he does. But again, it's proximity first, gauge reaction, then a controlled meet–and–greet with turning the dogs.

Based on dogs having positive reactions, they can greet face to face or they can be let off their leash to interact freely with each other. You stay close and watch the interactions and make sure that everything is playful and that no one is getting aggressive. Even if things are going very well, I still recommended stepping in and blocking to control the excitement level. If you see the excitement level escalate while they play, for example if you see them get up to Level #3 very quickly and then #4 and #6 and #7, then I would bring it back down to Level #1 and let them start over.

Practice that several times. Level #6 or #7 is a good challenge, but that means they are knocking on the door of #8, #9 or even Level #10. At that point, it's hard to stop them. You can't break their focus because they are in the zone. They don't hear commands anymore. It's like a baseball player who's got the bases loaded in the bottom of the ninth and the crowd is going crazy and he's so locked into the pitcher and focusing on the ball, that he can't even hear 35,000 fans screaming.

We do not want dogs in that zone.

If they pursue at that point with a behavior we don't like, we won't be able to stop it. And that is not willful disobedience; it's simply a dog being in the zone. Being in the zone doesn't imply aggression. They could be fixated on a toy or bone or they may want to run and play with the neighbor's dog.

Recognizing the escalation from calm to excitement and monitoring those levels of excitement is very important. Give them 30 to 45 seconds of play and break them up. Step in, block, and get back to a calm place. Give yourself five to ten seconds of calm and let them go again. It's almost like refereeing a boxing match. Break them up, let them regain their composure and back in they go. You can step in anytime you see an infraction or an escalation to a higher, undesirable level.

It's a lot easier to bring a dog down to Level #1 from Level #3 or #4 than from a higher level. As I stated before, once they get into Levels #8, 9 or 10, it's very difficult to bring them back. Then you actually have to pull on collars and physically remove them.

We do not want to let it get to that point.

By controlling the situation before it gets to that point, we are setting the rules right away, and making mental impressions for the dog that there's only a certain level of excitement that's allowed. This way, they are allowed to play, but they aren't allowed to exceed a certain level of excitement.

I've been asked if blocking makes dogs think they are not allowed to play. It's a good question, and my answer is: it's all about timing.

Shamus is trained to monitor the behavior of other visiting dogs to my home, and he is very good at his job. If we block relaxed interactions between dogs, then we are telling them to stay away from each other. But when we block them at a close to constant level of excitement, we're telling them that this is where the line is drawn. By practicing this on a regular basis, it becomes normal. So when our dogs get into a situation that is not controlled as we would like, they are already used to us stepping in, and they know how to react.

We practice these moves so we are able to perform them during an unforeseen event. We build muscle memory and improve our proficiency. When I use the meet–and–greet procedure in my home, it's a constant. This is what we do every time *any* dog comes in. If I didn't follow this procedure for puppies or dogs that I knew were stable, then I would only be putting Shamus behind the door when I thought there might be a problem. That energy will be detected by him, and create a trigger when he is put in that position. By being behind the door for every dog that comes in, it's simply the way we do things. Plus, Shamus has to show relaxed behavior in close proximity to the other dog before I open the door. That can be a challenge because the door provides a restrictive barrier and potentially more excitement.

But Shamus generally relaxes very quickly when put behind the door. Through cause and effect, he knows he will get what he wants with calm behavior, rather than excited behavior.

Repeating situational events will condition your dog on how to respond during future interactions.

Welcome to the World of Puppies and Rescue

This section discusses some of the major points of dealing with a new or rescue dog. We naturally want to smother a new dog with affection, but they will need time to build confidence and trust. The initial few months in our households are a very impressionable period, and we owe it to our new pals to get them started on the right paw.

Interactions with Dogs

If your puppy is the only dog in the household, limit their interactions with other dogs until they have been fully vaccinated. Consult your veterinarian about health issues surrounding other dog interactions.

When integrating a new puppy—or any new dog— meet–and–greets should be done on neutral ground. Even doing them outside the house or just down the street is a bit better than doing them in the home. Dogs are generally more receptive when territory is not in play.

The best procedure to introduce a new dog to resident dog(s) starts with proximity exercises. Each human will handle one dog. From across the street, let the dogs see each other. Start walking each dog in oval patterns, like the shape of an ice rink. The dogs should cross at the "center ice" spot. Notice each dog's body language as they pass each other. Correct any deep stares or growls by using blocking techniques.

Fixation is not permitted during a new greeting. If everything seems okay, make the ovals smaller and smaller until the dogs are in close proximity. Try to limit face–to–face greetings. It's best to manually turn the new dog around and allow the resident dog to sniff. Then, reverse positions and allow the new dog to sniff. If there are still no visible signs of tension, they can greet face–to–face. Keep that greeting short and sweet, and then just start walking the dogs side by side for about 15 to 20 minutes.

Allow the resident dog to enter the home first, and then bring in the new dog. Watch for any signs of tension or territoriality. Keep the dogs on their leashes until you are comfortable they can be let off. Always closely monitor interactions between integrated dogs until there is an established trust. If any incidents arise that cause a real fight, don't panic. Get behind the dogs and pull their back legs out. Separate immediately and call your trainer.

Puppy Proofing

New puppies are very curious. That's their job! They will explore their new world and in the process they will probably get into a lot of mischief.

Since we're always looking to set a dog up for success, start by confining your puppy to small areas of the house. Begin with a room or two, and always keep the dog in sight. There are some obvious things that will interest your puppy in your home. Shoes and articles of clothing will be particularly interesting to them because they smell like the humans of the house. Soft toys that belong to children will seem just like their soft, puppy toys. Try to remove or raise as many loose items as possible so the puppy has less opportunity to do wrong. Watch out for chewing of wood, wicker, and fabric. Other things to watch from a safety standpoint are wires and plants.

Puppy Meets Crate

Using a crate should be a positive experience for your dog. The first thing you want to do is reduce the size of the internal space with a divider. This should come with the crate. Only give the dog enough room to barely lie down and stretch out.

Dogs generally do not want to go potty in the space they occupy. By reducing the space, it helps to develop bladder control. If you give them the whole crate, they will potty on one side and rest on the other.

When introducing your dog to the crate, make sure it starts off positively. A puppy is very impressionable and it's important to give them the best chance for success. Set up the crate before the puppy arrives. Assembly may spook them a little.

Start by sitting with your dog near the crate and a treat. Then, put the treat right outside the crate. Then, put it just inside the crate so it only has to stick its head in. After that, place the treat a little further in so that it goes in with its front paws. Then, place the treat toward the back of the crate so it has to go all the way in. Do not close the door on the puppy right away.

Let it go in and out of the crate several times on its own. When it comes time to close the door, the puppy may whine, bark or cry. It is very important not to take it out. Let it work things out. Don't feel sorry for your puppy. It needs to feel your stability, not your pity. Plus if you remove the puppy when it carries on, you are teaching it how to get what it wants in a negative way. Every dog is different, but sometimes it's helpful to cover the crate with a blanket to make the dog feel more secure. It can also be helpful to put an unlaundered item of your clothing in the crate. They have your scent and it can be comforting. Use something like a T–shirt that you don't mind getting ruined. I would also advise against dog beds or anything that might be costly to replace or difficult to wash. Start with some old towels. They are easy to clean and it doesn't matter if they get chewed up a little. I know far too many people that have had an expensive dog bed soiled or destroyed within a few days.

Teaching Potty Training

The crate cycle is a guideline. It cannot be followed exactly to the minute. Maintain the best schedule possible, and use the puppy journal to document potty activity.

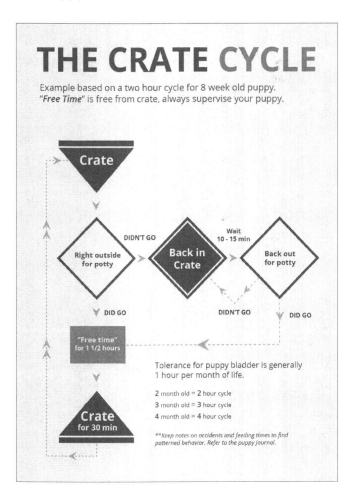

THE CRATE CYCLE

Example based on a two hour cycle for 8 week old puppy.
"Free Time" is free from crate, always supervise your puppy.

Crate

Right outside for potty — DIDN'T GO → **Back in Crate** → Wait 10 - 15 min → **Back out for potty**

DID GO

DIDN'T GO

DID GO

"Free time" for 1 1/2 hours

Tolerance for puppy bladder is generally 1 hour per month of life.

2 month old = **2** hour cycle
3 month old = **3** hour cycle
4 month old = **4** hour cycle

Crate for 30 min

**Keep notes on accidents and feeding times to find patterned behavior. Refer to the puppy journal.

The Puppy Journal

This is a good model for documenting your dog's potty activity. It helps to form patterns so you can more accurately predict potty behavior. If the dog has an accident in the house and you do not catch them in the act, you can't reprimand it. They will not associate the reprimand with the accident unless they are actually doing it at the time you point it out.

A reprimand should be delivered with a firm tone in a voice of displeasure. Your puppy does not understand the words you say, so it really doesn't matter. What matters is the inflection in your voice.

Do not rub your dog's face in the potty.

Take them immediately outside if you catch them, just in case they have to finish. If it was a number two, you can move it outside to the general area where you want the dog to go. Then, next time you take the dog outside, walk them around the other potty and see if they smell it. That might help them associate where they are supposed to go.

A Daily Sample

During the first few weeks of potty training, the puppy journal can be a very useful tool. With proper planning, you should be spending the first five to seven days with your puppy. This will allow you to follow this type of cycle as closely as possible.

In the first week of potty training, minutes matter. The dog will most likely be okay with a three or four-hour cycle during the day if you are at work and they are crated. During the first two to three weeks, they should not be asked to hold it longer than four hours. Accidents in the first month are generally a result of human error, as dogs need time to understand the process. After a month, and in many cases before, the dog is up to a four–hour cycle and sleeping through the night.

The sample below is based on the first week, and can be adjusted to the individual dog. The notes should answer some questions that usually arise.

6:45 a.m.	Outside Number 1
7:00 a.m.	Breakfast
7:15 a.m.	Outside Number 1 and 2
9: 00 a.m.	Accident Number 1 (This could have been avoided if the dog was in the crate at that time per the crate cycle.)
11:00 a.m.	Outside Number 1
12:15 p.m.	Back in crate
12:30 p.m.	Outside for Number 1
12:35 p.m.	Lunch
12:55 p.m.	Accident Number 2 (Dog went 15 minutes after breakfast, waiting 20 after lunch tells us that 15 is the limit for now. The digestion time will increase over the first few months.)
2:00 p.m.	Back in crate
2:30 p.m.	Outside, nothing, so back in the crate
2:45 p.m.	Outside Number 1
4:15 p.m.	Dog should go back in crate about this time, but happens to be sleeping. We can let them sleep where they are and then take them right out when they wake up, which in this example is 5 p.m.
5:00 p.m.	Outside Number 1

6:30 p.m.	Dinner
6:45 p.m.	Outside Number 1 and 2
9:00 p.m.	Accident Number 1 (Waited a little long and didn't put dog back in the crate. Sometimes it can be hard to put the dog back in the crate because the family is enjoying time with the new dog.)
11:00 p.m.	Outside Number 1
3:00 a.m.	Outside Number 1 (You can go four hours at night.)

The Ebb–and–Flow of Breaking a Comfort Zone

Once a dog begins to pass through its puppy phase, or in the case of rescue dogs or ones with special needs, there are desensitization and counter–conditioning exercises that we can employ to help a dog through difficult times. This is where I refer back to the two major schools of thought: Many Alpha trainers will challenge the dog repeatedly in a very short amount of time. This technique of induced exposure is called "flooding." The idea is that the dog will eventually accept the situation.

I used this technique when I first started training. It often worked during demonstrations, but in some cases, I wasn't seeing enough forward progress. I realized that the dogs just had no energy left to react. I didn't like that. So I looked for some answers.

I follow several dog discussion forums with many professional trainers. I thought I could learn some better techniques for these cases. I specifically read threads from the R+ forums. Many discussions seemed to favor very little exposure to triggers, preferring to allow dogs to avoid them altogether. I kept reading other threads and found more of the same in most cases.

This is the opposite of flooding; it's like a placid lake. There were also a lot of suggestions to medicate dogs. While I believe that some cases absolutely require medication, I also believe that it's become too much of a go–to option.

Just as personal growth requires getting out of our comfort zone, we must look at a challenging situation with our dogs from a similar perspective. Over–coddling a dog allows it to hide from its insecurities instead of facing them. The Doggyality Method emphasizes compromise, and it couldn't be more demonstrative than in this case of an unstable dog.

I will challenge an unstable dog and encourage them to get through the experience on their own. If I see the dog is becoming too stressed, in most cases, I will allow them to retreat. They are generally not allowed to run away and hide, but they do get breaks from induced exposures to triggers. When the dog has stabilized, we try again. As long as the dog is progressing we keep trying to move forward. If the dog is struggling with the next level, we regain confidence by dropping back to the last success point and rebuilding from there.

While I've made reference to the style of flooding and a placid lake, I refer to my style as ebb–and–flow.

But It's A Rescue

I've seen many cases in which an owner spoils a new rescue dog to make up for a difficult past. Although this sounds reasonable to us as humans, dogs receive this energy as uncertain.

The first week is such an impressionable time for a dog entering a new environment. They are generally a little insecure for the first several days, which is reasonable.

While we may think that giving them some human food is a good idea, it's setting a precedent that says it's okay to come into our space while we're eating.

When the dog adjusts to the environment and becomes secure, they will start exhibiting more brazen behavior. We may wonder why the dog won't leave us to eat, and may get frustrated. We must remember that we started all this by feeding the dog human food. They will be just fine with their kibbles from day one. If they don't eat for a few days, they will not starve. If we start adding things into the food to encourage them to eat, they will expect those things to always be in the food.

A rescue dog needs our strength, not our pity.

Some people feel like this tough love approach is wrong. We love to humanize, and equate dog life to human life. Okay, let's do that and see what it reveals. For example, a family has a child and they decide to adopt a second one. Let's assume that the adopted child's quality of life has not been as good as the resident child. It's the first evening and everyone sits at the table to a lovely dinner of chicken and vegetables. The adopted child says that he doesn't want chicken and veggies; he wants a fast food burger. What do you do?

I have prompted this scenario to hundreds of clients. Most of them say that they would direct the child to eat the dinner they have provided. This is setting boundaries and looking out for the best interest of that child's development. Why should it be any different for our dogs?

Doggyality Is Not Just for Dogs! Welcome to *Humanality 101*

By Marie Hallock (Las Cruces, NM)

Two-thousand-fourteen was a great year for our dogs and our family. Larry Fine came to our house as we have a problematic pit that really is a big teddy bear, but on occasion he gets angry and growls. That can be scary for us, but when we found Doggyality we learned to handle our dogs with more ease and confidence.

The afternoon Larry came to our house, I suggested he go out with the kids and the dogs. We were open to all that could happen that day and it started out on a very good note. The big dogs HarleyQuinn (boxer/pit mix) and Cali (red nose) went out the door with the kids and their new, fearless leader.

Honestly, we were at wits end and I was wondering how well things would go for the dogs. Little did I know that what also needed fine-tuning was the human element. I went outside to check on the group and lo and behold both of the dogs were clipped to Larry's belt and they were being so good.

Larry worked with us for five hours that day and it was like a light bulb turned on and the brain engaged.

We had been working more on establishing an emotional connection rather than confidence. All of our pets had been rescued from bad circumstances, and we were feeling sorry for them rather than giving them that confident, safe feeling that they need in order to be happy and healthy dogs.

HarleyQuinn has come light years from the dog we rescued. She came from an abusive past of baiting and breeding, so she was scared at first, but now we can let people in the house without any drama and she sometimes sits on the couch and just waits, knowing she is safe. Recently I had her outside in the backyard while I was cleaning up the kitchen. I could see her through the window and suddenly she jumped to her feet, barking. I immediately went outside and saw a man that sprays the yards here in our subdivision. The dog didn't charge or even get close enough to touch him; she just got behind me and I explained to him she didn't really like baseball hats and he took it off.

I always put my leg in front of her now to block when she is nervous and she immediately redirects her attention to me. If you had seen her in the beginning you wouldn't believe the change! She also follows me around with a broom; something she would have never done before. Through the techniques Larry taught us, she is now calm and isn't fearful she will be struck.

Cali is no longer the bullyboy he once was. At first, he was very good after the sessions, but then we had some slippage. We were still keeping him in the room because he liked to challenge my son who had grown weary of the situation.

These days, Cali and my son have a wonderful relationship. When a new person comes to the house he is slowly introduced, but he is good with folks now. My nephews and nieces sit on the couch with him and snuggle. We are having people over again and it feels really good.

Our family is all about rescue and we have been able to overnight other dogs without any altercations. Transporting, overnighting and fostering are all easier when your doggyality is shining through.

Cali is becoming the dog he always deserved to be. HarleyQuinn is so happy and content. I realize that we couldn't have done it without growing ourselves. The result is that our family—including Cali and HarleyQuinn—is now living in an atmosphere of peace and love.

Let Sleeping Dogs Lie

Many dogs have motion, sound, and proximal sensitivities. This is reasonable behavior. We also react when we hear or see something that startles us. Reactions of dogs are often misinterpreted. If we move into a resting dog's space, they may respond with a low growl or lip curl. That behavior can be considered guarding their territory, when most of the time they're just trying to communicate that they would like to be left alone. How would you feel if you were napping and somebody invaded your personal space? The warning signals must be recognized and accepted.

The expression "let sleeping dogs lie" comes to mind here. It probably came to be for a good reason. Respect your dog.

Every Dude Has a Past

Remember Dude? My "buddy?" He had some tough times before I found him. It was pretty hard not to feel sorry for him. But that's exactly what needed to be done. Dude *had* some tough times, and they were in his past. Now, in the comfort of my home, he was safe and starting fresh. For Dude to move forward, he needed strength, not pity. What he needed was stable energy with someone he could trust.

When we feel sorry for a dog, we put out negative energy.

Dogs don't understand English, and unlike humans, they don't have the capacity for reason and logic. So to say in a soft tone of voice that it's going to be okay is not only a waste of time; it's counterproductive.

A human would consider this behavior compassionate and reassuring. For a dog, that kind of energy feels unstable, and a dog will remain insecure. From my experience, petting him at that point would be received as affection and validate the dog's unstable state of mind.

There is a good amount of debate on this point in the dog training community. Many believe that comforting a dog during instability is positive. I can agree that when a dog spends enough time in a positive environment, affection can become a real comfort.

But in most cases I've monitored that use medication and all positive reinforcement, progress is slow, at best. While some cases certainly require behavior meds, I believe that challenging a troubled dog to break its comfort zone more often allows that dog more possibilities to overcome anxiety.

I've seen repeated evidence that this ebb–and–flow technique produces significant improvement within a shorter period of time. However, this approach is still a work in progress, and it will still take time and patience for a dog to really let go of stress or trauma. In this regard, a dog is no different than a human.

But I am happy to report that Dude has adjusted very well.

Empathy and Allelomimetic Behaviors

Empathy is the ability to understand and share the feelings of another. We've all experienced empathetic gestures from our dogs. They often attempt to comfort us when we are sick or upset. They stay close, looking a bit somber, and sometimes they even bring us one of their toys, thinking that it may please us.

Empathy is shared in positive experiences as well. If I cheer for a sports team, my dogs sometime share in that excitement.

The two most meaningful experiences of empathy I ever witnessed in a dog came from my Pit Bull, Shamus.

The first case occurred when he met a dog named Braxton that came from the Animal Control shelter in Philadelphia. Braxton's background was unknown, but he had significant anxiety and phobia issues. His owners are clients and they called me to see what they should do. They had just fallen in love with him, but they were scheduled for a vacation. They weren't sure he would be there when they got back.

I figured a week or ten days with me would do this dog some good so we agreed that they would adopt him and I would keep him at my house to work with him until they returned. Braxton was very nervous and was looking for a place with cover for security. When I bring an anxious dog in for the first time, I don't allow them to hide. They don't have to come near me if they don't want to, but they have to deal with it. Dealing with it simply means they can't go under a bed or table. They have to find a place to relax, even if it's in the corner.

Braxton paced around, not wanting anything to do with me. I gave him his space. After 10 to 15 minutes, he settled. As soon as Braxton lied down, Shamus approached and stood over him. He was providing security and comfort, but only after Braxton showed relaxation. Shamus stayed with his new friend for almost a half an hour. Once he left that space, I knew Braxton was stable. I calmly approached and Braxton accepted me with a sniff. Shamus told Braxton he could trust me. The two have been buddies ever since.

Shamus and Braxton: My Four-Legged Nurse

After I had a minor motorcycle accident, I needed to rest for several days. Shamus knew I was hurt and stayed close by. He waited for permission to come on to my bed. I wasn't sure if I should bring him up, but I wanted to cuddle with my buddy. I called him up but he was hesitant. He went around to the other side of the bed and jumped up from there, avoiding any close proximity to my leg. This went on several times throughout the day when I had to get up and then return to bed. I would prop up some pillows around my leg to keep it still and comfortable. Shamus would watch me each time. Then, one time he jumped on the bed, threw the pillows around my leg on the floor, and laid there in place of them. He didn't move until I was ready to get up again. This was not only empathetic behavior, but also allelomimetic.

Monkey See, Monkey Do

Allelomimetic behavior is a fancy term for mimicry. Dogs regularly copy behavior. Barking, playing, and running are some of the prominent examples in the average household. When dogs chase running children around the house, most assume that the dog is acting on its instincts to herd. While that may be the case sometimes, it is just as likely the dog is copying the child's behavior. This also correlates to the energy and body language of humans and a dog's instinctual, responsive behavior.

Roger Abrantes at the Ethology Institute Cambridge says, "Allelomimetic behavior is not restricted to animals of the same species. Animals of different species who live together show allelomimetic behavior regularly. Dogs are good body language readers and tend to respond to certain behaviors of their owners without needing further instruction. An alerted owner triggers his dog's alertness more often than the opposite."

While the copied behavior can sometimes be the result of a stimulus, allelomimetic behavior often works the opposite way.

I was once asked to do an evaluation for a rescue organization. I went to the holding facility and there was a row of kennels with roughly 15 dogs in the hall. I asked the staff to exit the area because I noticed right away that the dog in question was looking at the staff members with uncertainty and showing clear signs of anxiety. They were lovely people and experienced, but this was an abuse case and they understandably felt sorry for the dog.

All the dogs were barking and unreceptive. Once the hall was clear, I sat on the floor in the center of the hall and practiced some breathing exercises. Within a minute or so, one dog stopped barking, then another and another until the hall was quiet. This took roughly five minutes. This calm allowed me to connect with the abused dog and see that there was a strong likelihood for a successful rehabilitation.

New Kid on the Block

Another way of using allelomimetic behavior to our advantage is when we have a new dog in an environment with a resident dog. The new dog may be a puppy, foster or rescue. It doesn't know the lay of the land and will not understand why it's been moved there. That kind of uncertainty is stressful for a dog. We can use the resident dog to teach the new dog basic commands, such as which door it picks to request a potty break. This technique can also work with more advanced behavior.

Several years ago, I had a foster named Teddy. He was timid, and didn't know very much in the way of commands. He was nervous from the transition and wasn't taking food treats, which is common.

The next day, I wanted to see if I could teach him some basic commands, thinking the mental stimulation would be good for him. He seemed interested in the food, but any motion toward him would cause him to pull back, even if it was to give him food.

Then I started performing some basic commands with one of my dogs. Cassie was spot on and got her treats, which started to pique Teddy's interest. He watched her intently as she did her repetitions. He then walked right over and joined in. Within a half–hour, he was becoming proficient in sit, down, and stay.

Teddy was a little guy who could jump, so the next day I introduced him to an agility bar. Cassie always had a problem with the jump bar, even if it was just a few inches off the ground. I wasn't expecting her to participate. Teddy took treats near the object, then through the object with no cross bar. He then took a treat off of the installed cross bar. He was following my luring well, and in just a few minutes he was jumping over the bar. I raised the bar incrementally, with continued success. Then, uninvited and out of nowhere, Cassie came running over and jumped the bar for the first time ever. Looks like the student just became the teacher!

Touch–Testing and the Feeding Ritual

While puppies and new rescues are so cute and cuddly, it's important not to over coddle either of them. If your puppy seems nervous or insecure, it will reap rewards if you let it work things out by itself.

Assuming the dog is not injured and doesn't need to potty, don't pet or pick it up in attempts to calm it. I know it is counter–intuitive, but trust me on this. It's also important that the dog have a sense of autonomy. This is a good preventative measure against separation anxiety, which can develop if the dog is given too much affection and not enough time in their own space. That can be in their crate during the crate cycle, and it can also happen just resting at a distance from humans. If you regularly infringe on your dog's space while they are resting, it may become more needlessly protective of its space.

There is plenty of time to provide affection. Just understand that affection is validation. So if the puppy jumps up and you pet them, you're telling them you like it when they jump. Try to use affection as a reward for positive reinforcement.

Dogs learn by cause and effect.

It's okay to play with your puppy, of course, but there is also a time for calm. During calm and cuddle time, affection can be provided. This associates reward with relaxed behavior, and the puppy is receptive to touch when they are relaxed.

It's also a good time to use the dog's name so it will recognize it. You will want to perform touch–tests with your new puppy on their pads and paws, all around the head, ears and snout. Touch the puppy's tail and belly. Because a dog will be handled by various humans throughout its life, it's good to get it used to it early. This will help you bond as well.

Food is among the most valuable things in a dog's life. Some dogs feel the need to guard its food or other resources. Feeding time should be a structured interaction for a new dog. Before we even establish an everyday feeding routine, we should do a few food tests.

It's a good idea to hand feed the first few meals. This is useful in establishing a patient approach to food. It's also a great way to bond, as our scent is associated with the food. Perhaps most important, it conditions the dog that having us around its food is positive.

The next few meals we can put some kibble in the bowl. Then, we put our hand around the bowl, even *in* the bowl, while the dog eats. The next exercise is interrupting the meal by removing the bowl. We will place the bowl back down if the dog remains calm. This can be repeated a few times each meal over a few days.

At this point, we can start the regular daily feeding routine. The dog should remain about six feet away from the feeding area until we release it. After the bowl is placed on the ground, the dog should maintain eye contact with us and then we can step away and point to the bowl. The eye contact is important, as the dog is then taking direction instead of just plowing toward the bowl. With the proper feeding routine, a dog will calmly approach its food upon release. This keeps emotion at bay during food time. As noted in other examples, emotion is what leads to reactive behavior.

It's A Family Affair!

On the next page, you will find the Doggyality Exercise Chart. This is a very useful tool to keep household members accountable for doing the exercises. It is particularly useful for families with children.

Replace the names on the top line of the chart with the names of your own family members. At the beginning of the week, everybody should list his or her respective goals. At the end of the week, fill in the totals. If the children's goals are reached, maybe the parents will reward them as motivation. Involving children in the training process is not only good for their relationship with your dog. It also provides developmental benefits.

Dog and child interactions teach responsibility and compassion, and can be very therapeutic and validating. You can fill in the boxes with color markers that match each participant or use color stickers that will further engage your children.

EXERCISE CHART

Exercise chart is used to monitor your interactions & activity training with your dog.

	Jack	Jill	John	Jane	Joe	Jenn
Goals:	21	21	21	21	21	21
Totals:	22	22	23	18	26	17

	Monday	Tuesday	Wednesday	Thursday	Friday	Saturday	Sunday
Sit							
Down							
Stay							
Feeding Ritual							
Impulse Control							

Part Three:
Happy Human, Happy Dog

Happy Dog, Happy Human?

Like many other ideas and practices, I like to look at things from the other side. There is a widely used saying of "happy dog, happy human." I'm not sure where I first heard this, but I've since heard it used hundreds of times, and used it myself during the first few years of my training.

Bringing personal growth into the equation gave me the opportunity to view this concept another way. As I found out more and more about the correlation of human energy and dog behavior, I reversed the saying to "happy human, happy dog." This resonated well, and was in the line of thought that describes the focus of my method.

Taking on personal growth challenges builds confidence and positive energy. These are the two most important things in rehabilitating a dog with anxiety, phobia or aggression. They are also among the most important things when dealing with puppy behavior. Being more satisfied with who we are yields sanguine momentum, which is to say when we get in touch with who we are, we can have—and maintain—a more hopeful perspective. That state of mind yields better results from better decisions—not just in dog training, but in life.

Who Is Your Dog?

Most of the time, we try to get dogs to adjust to our world and expect them to comply. I think we should be more focused on what *we* can do to help *them* adjust better. We just assume that dogs know their role in our household, but they really don't. How could they? They are programmed much differently. Therefore, our communication needs to be clear and our dedication to a proper relationship must include clear boundaries as much as it does affection. That means limits as much as it does rewards. This helps our dogs to relax more.

They enjoy taking direction; it makes their life less stressful.

It's also important to recognize that our dogs have unique doggyalities. Sure, there are breed characteristics, but they are individuals. For example, I've seen retrievers that don't retrieve.

As humans, we have high expectations of our dogs. I've seen hundreds of puppy cases, and it's almost as if people expect their dogs to become furry little robots that can be programmed to behave as we wish. On top of that, some owners expect it to happen within a few weeks.

This is just unrealistic.

We rely heavily on operant conditioning because dogs learn through cause and effect. They don't have the same logic and reason that we humans do, and we need to remember that. It would be great if we could just explain it to them like we do with people, but we can't. Instead, we have to show them through interactions. This requires repetition, consistency, and a relaxed state of mind. We become impatient easily. We get frustrated over what we perceive as non–compliance, when it's usually improper communication.

Since most dog communication is nonverbal, we must rely on energy and body language.

Energy Shifts and Standoffs

Energy shifts occur as we regain control of our "zen" state. For most of us, the ability to create that requires a lot of practice. We have to essentially let go in order to hold on.

Does that even make sense? It does, as long as we're taking it figuratively.

For me, becoming more proficient at controlling my behavior only started when I got better at controlling my emotions. Behavior is the manifestation of emotion. Once I learned that, which surely didn't happen overnight, I wanted to progress further. I believed that if I could truly internalize emotion, there would be no outbursts. During several attempts at this, I thought I was doing pretty well, and pretty quickly.

But I found out a few weeks later that I was not internalizing; I was suppressing. It would have been ideal if I could have held my emotions in check and channel them in a constructive manner. But that was not the case. I would keep myself together for some big things and feel proud for doing so, and then lose it over something so petty it was just plain embarrassing.

Controlling our emotions can be like putting an inflatable ball in a pool. If you push the ball just under the surface, it gently pops back up. If you push the ball down to the bottom of the pool, it comes up with more force. So when I needed to temporarily store some feelings just under the surface, I was pushing them too far down.

Over time, I have gotten better and better at this, and life has become easier. Since I have learned to genuinely internalize my emotions, I have experienced increasingly positive responses from my family, friends, clients—and dogs.

There are times when I can feel energy shifts inside my body. It is like getting the chills in slow motion. It starts as a sensation at a specific point and then moves throughout the body. My output at that point is pure.

This is an ongoing exercise. Most days I succeed, and sometimes I fail. I don't let it get me down; I just try to do better the next time I am in a similar situation.

Energy Shifts with Dogs

When I feel an energy shift, I get immediate, positive reactions from dogs. Sometimes the energy shift happens to the dog first and I follow suit. That is a rarer occurrence, but it happens.

My first energy shift occurred with Cassidy, although I had no idea of its significance at the time. While I was unaware of the first several experiences, which were infrequent, they informed my future work with many different types of dogs.

The most common major shifts take place during behavior disorder work, like anxiety, phobia and aggression. I've been in standoffs with aggressive dogs for up to 27 minutes. If a dog confronts me, I hold my ground. Giving up space will empower the dog, and moving into the dog's space at that point can present a challenge. By simply holding my ground and staying relaxed, it diffuses many situations that would otherwise escalate.

When a dog voluntarily stops barking and backs away from its position, I calmly move in a few steps. When the dog backs off, I will occupy about the same amount of space that it just vacated. This is a gesture the dog will understand.

During these standoffs, my energy and the dog's are floating around the room together. If each of us can get to a point of relaxation at the same time, our energies will synchronize. I equate it to Bluetooth. When we are synched up, we can communicate just fine, but we have to connect first.

This is admittedly one of the hardest things to accomplish. Even if a dog is six feet away and leashed, if it is growling and bearing teeth, it's not easy to stay relaxed. Imagine doing it without the leash.

The relaxed nature of the standoff builds trust. I've had equally long greetings with anxiety/phobia cases. I like to try to get into the house further in these situations. Being around the door is a stress point. I find that getting into the living room to sit and chat brings a more stable set up. As soon as I feel my energy shift, the dog stops barking. They will generally sniff with the head up, showing interest. I remain relaxed and make no gestures. I wait for the dog to be sure that they are comfortable, and let them come into my space. This is an important distinction between dealing with anxiety/phobia issues versus those that are about dominance and territoriality.

Beryl Eismeier Learns To Do "Nothing"

We initially called Larry because of Luna, our eight–month old Corso, who we brought home at 12 weeks. We thought we had lavished enough love and attention and basic clicker training that we'd be okay with this large breed. She could do "Sit" and "Down" but if one of us suddenly entered a room, or if the doorbell rang, our sweet puppy became a menacing wild beast, barking, charging, jumping and crouching, hackles up, growling and stalking.

Neighbors walking their dogs were the worst trigger. If Luna was outside at the time and noticed, she'd bolt away at a staggering speed. Commands she knew had no meaning; we couldn't talk her down and she was getting too big to pick up and restrain. We had to do something!

On his first visit, we met Larry on the porch and he entered our foyer with little fanfare or introduction. It didn't matter because as usual, Luna exploded. Larry made no eye contact, spoke softly to us, and asked us to allow him to settle in and not to interfere. We waited. Luna did all her usual moves—barking and jumping, sniffing, then growling and retreating, springing back, and more growling. Her hair stood on end. Larry patiently stood there, looking at nothing, smiling a little, and occasionally sighed.

We just watched as he mesmerized Luna into quite a state. First, the barking ceased. Luna paced in the adjacent room, threw in an occasional whimper and whined at us. This went on for at least 20 minutes. Wide-eyed, we chuckled. Larry explained what was happening, and little by little we saw that he had essentially sucked the oxygen away from her flame. She sniffed him; approaching and retreating several times. Finally worn out, she downed herself off to the side. That was it. We did nothing but watch. Larry did "nothing." And it just kind of blew our minds.

We still use this method with new visitors and it works. It just does.

Stuck On Words

In my experience, word associations can create barriers. When I tell a client that their dog is insecure or unstable, their faces can tell quite a story. In this context, when I see a dog with real insecurity or an unstable state of mind, the words I use to describe the dog are not meant to be negative; they are simply the truth.

I have insecurities, and so do you. Everyone does! Recognition is a positive step forward. To automatically become unreceptive is a disservice to our dogs and ourselves. Unfortunately, I see this happen way too often.

I read several articles a day on dog behavior and I notice a lot of debate on dog training methodology, with opinions supporting and refuting every existing method. One of the pitfalls of any profession is to get stuck in a single method.

I'm a trainer that started with a good amount of forced submission, alpha rolls and strict pack mentality. Those techniques worked fine for me, but were difficult for the average dog owner to perform. I wanted to learn other ways because every dog is different, and needs to be treated as an individual.

If we try to solve issues using a preconceived notion, we are setting ourselves up for failure. A dog barks or growls for different reasons. Body language can be ambiguous to the untrained eye, and sometimes to the trained eye, as well. There are many resources available that can teach you how to deal with a particular behavior.

As I have shifted my methodology twice since starting my practice, I realize that there is always more to learn. Since I have developed a cognitive learning process for both dog and human, I have enjoyed watching my clients become more successful.

Warning: Three Words You May Not Want to Hear

I used some words in the preceding paragraph that many people don't care for. Though these days I only need to use a forced submission on a rare occasion, just seeing the word "submission" is troubling for many. Even though my methods are of a cognitive, non–physical nature, submission is a necessary aspect of dog training. Submission does not have to be forced; it can be commanded, and it can be voluntary.

Alpha doesn't fly, nor does pack mentality, with Positive Only training. It is commonly argued that pack mentality doesn't apply anymore, and the domestication of dogs has basically severed their ties to the wolf.

I contend that basic instinctual behavior remains in dogs.

Though I base my practice on positive technique, most animals—human and canine—respond to consequence. There is another one of those words. Does "consequence" make you think of physical rebuke or denial of needs? If it does, please realize that consequence is a tool to teach the dog how to get what they want in a proper manor. It's okay for a dog to want your affection, but it's not okay for them to jump on you or invade your space to get it. The consequence for that action is not providing the affection. When the dog settles and shows better manners, affection is provided as a reward for good behavior. If it is acceptable to you that your dog jumps on you at the door, please don't discredit them or discipline them for jumping on your guests. You have encouraged that behavior.

Dogs learn by cause and effect. Mental impressions cannot be made through cause without effect. There is no reward if there is no consequence.

Now here comes the mother of all controversial words in dog training: "Dominance." I dominate dogs on a daily basis. What kind of images does that create in your head?

Hold on to those as you read the next two sentences.

I dominate mentally, not physically.

Dominance is not about intensity;
it's about a stable state of mind.

Did those images just change? If so, you've shown the ability to open your mind to a word that just seconds ago you associated as a negative. That's the essence of counter–conditioning. Don't let words block you. Understand their context before rejecting them. Those words could turn out to be the impetus of a valuable growth experience.

Remember Wendy Kaplan from Ft. Lauderdale? Her story in the introduction demonstrates what can be accomplished with the cognitive process. We have had many outstanding conversations over the last few years, and she has helped bring out some of my softer side.

Wendy was once stuck on the word "submission." Through some spirited debate, we decided that changing the word "submission" to "compliance" was a good fit for Doggyality. And just recently, we decided to change the name of a space–control exercise I do from "No–Yes–No" to "Your Time, Our Time."

As I have continued to adjust my methods, I've learned the benefits of compromise, not just with technique, but with style.

Learn To Love Your Walk

Walking with your dog can be the most therapeutic time of your day. It's certainly when the two of you get to bond in a very meaningful way. A lot of people look at walking their dog as a chore. If the dog doesn't walk properly, then it's laborious and tires you out physically and mentally. But walking your dog should be an invigorating activity, not a depleting one.

Dogs benefit from the mental relaxation of a focused walk. A focused walk is not about the dog sniffing and exploring, or as I like to call it, "doggy social media."

Sniff, sniff.

"Lucy was here today."

Sniff, sniff.

"What's her status?"

"Well, I'll just go ahead and lift my leg to 'check in' on Dogsquare."

Should dogs be allowed to walk in front of us? It depends on the dog. When most dogs are out in front, they are in a leading state of mind. Their head is on a swivel; they are alert and aware. They're not relaxed; the body is rigid, and their ears are up. They are getting physical exercise, but they are not getting any release from the mind.

With the proper focused walk, a dog will walk at your side or behind you.

At first, it would need a four–foot leash to limit its movements and keep better control. A six–foot leash and beyond allows a dog too much slack, so in case it lunges or projects itself at something—dog, human or a leaf blowing across the ground—the dog will have two more feet of momentum, which is not desirable.

A shorter leash makes it that much harder for the dog to pull you with more force. Again, the more energy you have to expend to control the dog, the more you may wear down physically and mentally. Having the dog back at your side or behind you will allow the dog to fall into a more relaxed state of mind, where it won't have to be in a constant state of alert. This way, it can enjoy nature, and stay happy out on its walk.

The more time you build with quality, focused walking, the more it will become the norm. Dogs accept it and get the most out of it. By being out front, you're putting your dog in a state of mind that is different and more relaxed than it is used to by being the one out in front. So when they encounter other dogs, or humans, or something that is usually stimulating to them, they are less likely to be reactive because they are in a calmer state of mind. And if they do react, it's a lot easier to bring them down to a reasonable level and a more relaxed state of mind.

Remember our Level 1–to–10 scenario? A dog walking with a loose leash at your side or a step or two behind is a #1, nice and relaxed, with bouncy ears and a bouncy tail, head up, and with a waggle to the body. That tells you that your dog is in the zone.

There is a thing with humans called a "runners high," where after a certain amount of exercise the body produces endorphins that trigger a euphoric feeling. People say that exercise gives them more energy than it takes away. What is happening is this: a chemical process in the body is rewarding them for that exercise because the body needs it.

That's how I feel about my experiences with dogs. When you experience focused walking on a regular basis, you start to counter–condition obstacles like excitement around other dogs. Work on those procedures to meet–and–greet in a calmer manner. When our dog is in a receptive state, we are able to do that.

With its ears up and its head on a swivel in alert status, you are not starting off at Level #1; you're already at Level #5. As soon as your dog makes eye contact with another dog, it goes right up to Level #7. Once that happens, you have very little chance of bringing it back down before it goes up to a full blown Level #9 or #10.

Most of the time, that reaction prompts restraint, which causes tension. It's usually for play, not for any kind of aggression. But the frustration produces growls and barking that can simulate a seemingly aggressive response. When that happens with regularity, we may start to anticipate those types of reactions. When we see the triggers approaching, we start to tense up and pull hard on the leash. We grip it until our knuckles get white. Our body gets rigid and we brace ourselves for the impact or the force of the dog's reaction.

When we become tense like that, we wind up fueling the dog's tension. But if we can relax during that time and not anticipate a problem, we put out a better energy vibe. This will give our dogs better chances of success in their interactions during your walk.

Although we assume that we are walking our dogs for their benefit, shouldn't we also have a positive, energizing and/or relaxing experience? I definitely find that my days are better when I get quality walks with my dogs.

That's what this book is about: education, motivation and inspiration. I believe that this process—the Doggyality Method— can help you discover a happier self, leading the way to establishing a very meaningful relationship with your best friend.

CONCLUSION
When Personality Meets Doggyality

Take Five—Actually, Take Ten

I would like to offer you an exercise that I do every day, no matter what. I take ten minutes to myself. I do this three times a day. That's thirty minutes for me every day, guaranteed. I take my tens at different points throughout the day and for different reasons. I spend my tens in different ways. It all depends on the particular day. On a stressful day, my tens help center me. On a garden–variety day, my tens are often spent just sitting quietly. Practicing breathing and stretching exercises are good options as well. Sometimes, I call a friend and catch up a bit. Sometimes, I play backgammon on my phone. Whatever the choice, I make sure I get my tens. While I was writing this book, I took a lot of tens just playing with my dogs.

I used to take fives, but then I learned that tens are twice as good as fives.

I encourage you to take a ten, find your Zen, and see how your day improves.

Jenn Shaw Gets It

When we adopted our puppy Macy in March of 2014 we had no idea how to train a dog! A friend recommended we call Larry to come to our house and help us learn about Macy and figure out what she needed from us.

From the minute he walked in, Larry was able to tell that Macy is a very shy and timid dog. He sat down and chatted with us about his life and how he found this career—or rather this career found him. After a little while, he felt Macy was ready to learn and showed us some training tricks.

First, he taught us to take deep breaths and relax! It was huge!

Macy responded instantly and seemed happy to know that someone actually got her! We learned about blocking and keeping Macy away from things we didn't want her near. As Larry was training Macy he explained to us that he loved what he was doing with dogs and helping people understand who dogs really are and what they need. He decided that life was for living and doing something you love, so he re–routed his career path.

A few months after Larry had visited our house, my company went through a major change and I was miserable. I have three small children and I was snapping at them and basically spending all my time doing work and being annoyed when they interrupted me.

I thought back to Larry and how he not only taught us about our dog, but also a little about life. I decided to give notice at my job and I have never been happier. Larry not only taught us about how to be good dog owners, but also how to live life to the fullest. Since then, our quality of human and canine life has improved significantly.

Happiness is Cassidy's Ranch

After all is said and done; after all the dog–training techniques have been learned and personal introspection is at its peak, here is what I've learned:

Happiness is when *who you are* meets *who you want to be.*

For me, my ultimate vision of happiness and my goal for Doggyality is Cassidy's Ranch. This will be a privately funded facility with the purpose of impacting a larger audience to affect positive change on the adoptable pool of dogs.

Cassidy's Ranch will serve as a halfway house for rescue dogs with anxiety/phobia. The location will more than likely be in a southern state, possibly the Carolinas or Georgia. Transports originating in the South will be able to bring the dog to Cassidy's Ranch for a few weeks of rehabilitation. Then, the transport will resume. When they reach their new foster or adopter, their state of mind will be much improved. They will also come with written advice and instruction on how to keep each particular dog moving forward.

The extent to which Cassidy's Ranch can provide services will be a result of the success of the Doggyality business model. With enough resources, a larger scale operation would include a bigger facility and a dormitory. Staff may have options to live on the ranch. We can document the activities, and educational videos will be produced and provided to rescue organizations.

Happiness is when "who you are" meets "who you want to be."

If possible, all services and materials will be provided at no cost. Additionally, a section of the ranch could serve as a sanctuary for some of the cases that will not move forward with a good quality of life in the average household. Volunteers, rescuers, and trainers from near and far would be invited to learn through observation and participation.

Cassidy's Ranch will offer an environment of positive energy. It will serve as a spiritual retreat, providing rejuvenation of the mind and soul for all who visit—human and canine.

Every person who supports Doggyality contributes to this goal. Thank you.

Cassidy
2001–2010

ACKNOWLEDGMENTS

I would first like to acknowledge the encouragement and support of my family and friends. Mom and Dad, Janis Fine, Bruce Schildkraut, Jason Zatman, Reid Wagner, David Sunico and Carrie Hartman—you guys are the best.

I would also like to give a shout–out to fosters, transporters and volunteers in animal welfare. Your dedication has inspired me to do my best every day.

Thanks to Jeff and Yael Morgan for shining their light on me.

Thanks to Kristin Flagg, who has been my friend and colleague for several years. Through a client from her dog walking service, she introduced me to my dog, Shamus. For that alone, I'll love her always. Kristin is also a very talented musician and photographer. She is credited with numerous photographs in this book, including the cover photo. Kristin has combined her love of dogs and her artistic passion to create merchandise celebrating the canine/human bond. Please visit www.indigoskyworld.com.

Thanks to Lee Kancher, whose company Right Brain Group, has also been my right arm. Lee has truly gone above and beyond to help me, as he is a fellow dog lover who believes in what Doggyality is trying to accomplish. From design and implementation to marketing and site maintenance, my website is the product of Right Brain Group's dedication to quality. Lee is also credited with the cover design and graphics of this book. Please visit www.rightbraingroup.com

Choosing an editor was perhaps the most important decision I had to make. I had a great feeling about David Tabatsky right away. As a first–time writer, understanding the process was essential. David has guided me through every step. His expertise really shined during construction of the manuscript. He was able to help me fill in the missing elements and bring it all together. Thank you, David. Please visit www.tabatsky.com.

Last but not least, thanks to Wendy Kaplan, Marie Hallock, Alicia Harantschuk, Beryl Eismeier and Jenn Shaw. Thank you all for sharing your stories! Thank you too, Sara Shack and Dori Cohen, for allowing me to share the stories of Homer and Dude.

ABOUT THE AUTHOR

Since opening his first business—a car detailing service—when he was 16, Larry Fine has been an entrepreneur. Eventually, through the ups and downs he experienced with various enterprises, Larry, then in his 30's, realized the toll that this stressful lifestyle was taking and decided to focus more on quality of life.

Learning to live on less and enjoy the simple things was cathartic. It was at that point when his energy started to change, and projecting a positive outlook on life came naturally.

Falling backwards into dog training was the best thing that ever happened to Larry. He has always approached his business endeavors with gusto. He maintains his teaching schedule, volunteer commitments and production of educational materials, while continuing his journey of personal growth. Through his touring schedule and remote training program, Larry has serviced clients, recues, transports and other dog trainers across the country.

This is the first time in his life, he says, that "going all in" has been a healthy pursuit.

Larry resides in Bala Cynwyd, Pennsylvania, a suburb of Philadelphia, and has dedicated his life to helping dogs and humans live more fulfilled lives.

You can contact Larry Fine at:

Doggyality
P.O. Box 191
Merion Station, PA 19066
info@doggyality.com

Please visit www.doggyality.com

Made in the USA
Middletown, DE
30 May 2015